Current Chinese Economic Report Series

More information about this series at http://www.springer.com/series/11028

Industrial Economic Situation Analysis Team,
Institute of Industrial Economics, CASS
Editor

Summer Report of China Industrial Economic Situation Analysis (2016)

中国社会科学出版社
CHINA SOCIAL SCIENCES PRESS

Springer

Editor
Industrial Economic Situation Analysis Team,
Institute of Industrial Economics,
CASS
Beijing
China

ISSN 2194-7937 ISSN 2194-7945 (electronic)
Current Chinese Economic Report Series
ISBN 978-981-10-4689-6 ISBN 978-981-10-4690-2 (eBook)
DOI 10.1007/978-981-10-4690-2

Jointly published with China Social Sciences Press

The print edition is not for sale in China Mainland. Customers from China Mainland please order the print book from: China Social Sciences Press

Library of Congress Control Number: 2017942972

Printed on acid-free paper

This Springer imprint is published by Springer Nature
The registered company is Springer Nature Singapore Pte Ltd.
The registered company address is: 152 Beach Road, #21-01/04 Gateway East, Singapore 189721, Singapore

Preface

In the first half of the year 2016, the general characteristic of Chinese industrial economics was "stabilization with a tendency of slowing down and a limited recovery." The industrial structure continued to show the high-grade trend. The central region was the pacesetter, and the northeast region's industrial economic growth was feeble with the differentiation development inside. There was a sign of narrowing the gap of industrial growth rates among Beijing, Tianjin, and Hebei. The decreasing amplitudes of industrial export and industrial products' ex-factory price continued to narrow. The industrial enterprises' profits bounced back, and the inventory pressure was eased, but the tasks of overcapacity reduction still have a long way to go. Chinese industrial economic growth rate has been slowing down since 2010, and the first half of the year 2016 continued this trend. According to the results of model prediction, we predict that in the December 2016, the Industrial value-added growth rate above a designated scale would fall to 5.7%, and in June 2017, there is a high probability that the Industrial value-added growth rate above a designated scale would drop to 5.0%. In this condition, more efforts are needed in macroeconomic regulation to balance the steady growth and structural adjustment. On the one hand, it is necessary to pay careful attention to promoting supply-side structural reforms and the institutional mechanisms by which market should play a decisive role in the allocation of resources as proposed at the Third Plenary Session of the 18th Central Committee of the Communist Party of China, and get rid of institutional barriers to lay a solid foundation for the healthy development of the industrial economics. On the other hand, it is also necessary to maintain a steady economic growth, deepen the concept of "range control", and take effective measures in advance to deal with risks and challenges, but at the same time what calls for special attention is that drastic fluctuations of macroeconomic policies should be avoided so as to maintain the relative stability and continuity of macroeconomic policies.

Board of Editors

Host of Research Group

Prof. Huang Qunhui, Director of Institute of Industrial Economics, CASS
Zhang Qizi, Professor of Institute of Industrial Economics, CASS

Member of Research Group

Huang Yanghua, Jiang Feitao, Li Fangfang
Li Gang, Liang Yongmei, Wang Xiuli
Wang Yanmei, Wu Lixue Yuan Jingzhu, Yuan Lei, Zhang Hangyan, Zhang Yanfang

Writer of the Report

Zhang Hangyan, Wang Xiuli, Li Fangfang

Contents

List of Figures

List of Tables

Chapter 1
Analysis of Industrial Economics Operation in the First Half of the Year 2016

Hangyan Zhang

In the first half of the year 2016, China industrial economics showed a development trend towards stabilization. The development trend of manufacturing industry seemed better than mining industry. The northeastern region witnessed an industrial recovery. The decreasing amplitude of industrial export continued to narrow and the industrial enterprises' profits bounced back. The industrial profits of such raw materials as coal, steel and non-ferrous materials continued to show a recovering growth. The growth rate of industrial investment slowed down. The decreasing amplitude of industrial products' ex-factory prices continued to narrow and the inventory pressure was eased, but the task of overcapacity reduction still had a long way to go.

1.1 Overall Analysis of Industry

China industrial economics presented a trend towards stabilization. In the first half of the year 2016, the added value of industrial enterprises above a designated scale grew at the rate of 6.0%, 0.1 percentage point down against the year of 2015; in the first quarter, the growth rate was 5.8%, 0.3 percentage point lower than the second quarter's 6.1%. According to monthly data, the added value of industrial enterprises above a designated scale grew 5.4, 6.8, 6, 6 and 6.2% respectively in January and February, March, April, May and June, indicating a trend to stability since March. The industry continued to move towards high and mid grade. In the first half year, hi-tech industries and equipment manufacturing industry witnessed a year-on-year growth of 10.2 and 8.1% respectively, 4.2 percentage points and 2.1 percentage points higher than and accounting for 12.1 and 32.6% of the industrial

H. Zhang (✉)
Industrial Economic Situation Analysis Team, Institute of Industrial Economics, CASS, #5 Jianguomennei Street, 100732, Beijing, P.R. China

I.E.S.A.T. Institute of Industrial Economics, CASS (ed.), *Summer Report of China Industrial Economic Situation Analysis (2016)*, Current Chinese Economic Report Series, DOI 10.1007/978-981-10-4690-2_1

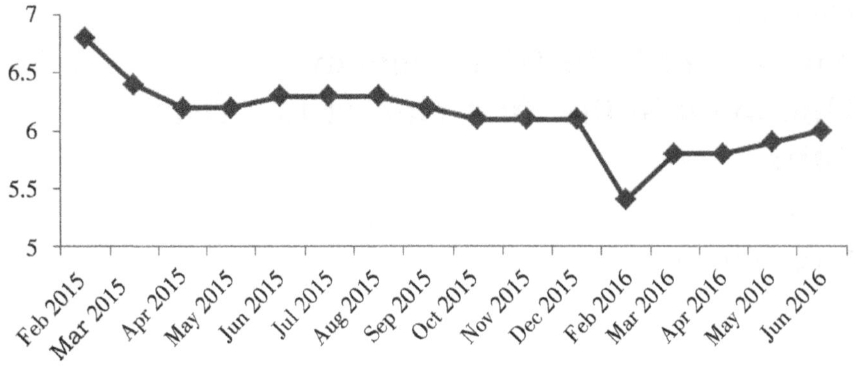

Fig. 1.1 Accumulative industrial value added growth rates above a designated scale since 2015. *Source* National Bureau of Statistics website

enterprises above a designated scale respectively, and 0.7 percentage point and 1.2 percentage points higher than the same period last year respectively (Fig. 1.1).

In terms of Industrial value added in three major industrial categories, a "reversal" trend (as illustrated in Fig. 1.2) appeared in the added value growth rates of such industries as manufacturing and mining as well as production and supply of electric power, heating power, fuel gas and water. In the first half of the year 2016, the added value of mining industry grew 0.1% on a year-on-year basis, 2.6 percentage points down against the year of 2015 and 2.0 percentage points down

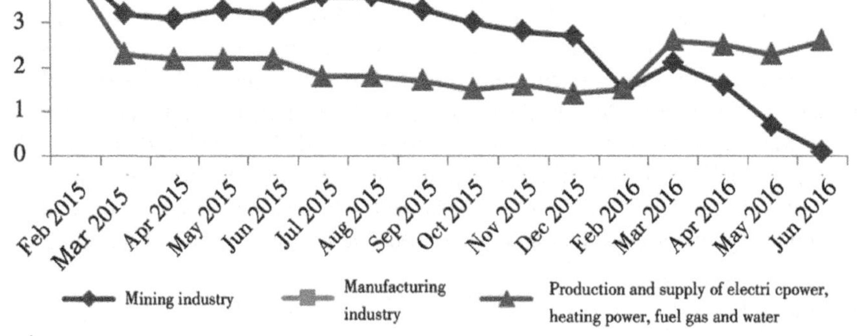

Fig. 1.2 Accumulative industrial value added growth rates above a designated scale of three major categories scale since 2015. *Source* National Bureau of Statistics website

against the first quarter of 2016; the manufacturing industry grew 6.9%, 0.1 percentage point down against the year of 2015 and 0.4 percentage point higher than the first quarter of 2016; and the production and supply of electric power, heating power, fuel gas and water grew 2.6%, 1.2 percentage points higher than the year of 2015 and flat with the first quarter of 2016. In terms of monthly growth of Industrial value added, in June 2016, the mining industry fell 2.4% year on year, 3.9 percentage points down against January and February; the manufacturing industry grew 7.2%, 1.2 percentage points higher than January and February; and the production and supply of electric power, heating power, fuel gas and water grew 4.0%, 2.5 percentage points higher than January and February.

In terms of Industrial value added growth in different regions, the industry in central region witnessed the fastest growth while the northwestern industry seemed feeble with the differentiation development inside. In June 2016, the Industrial value added of eastern region grew 6.7% year on year, 0.6 percentage point down against the same period last year; the central region grew 7.1%, 0.3 percentage point higher than the same period last year; and the western region grew 6.7%, 1.1 percentage points down against the same period last year. The Industrial value added in northeastern region dropped 1.1% year on year, a negative growth that occurred again following last month's recovery, indicating a feeble industrial recovery in the eastern region and the differentiation development inside northeastern industry. The Industrial value added of Jilin Province suffered a sharp decline after a three-month stable growth, and grew 5.8, 7.2 and 7.4% on a year-on-year basis in March, April and May respectively, exceeding the average industrial growth rate for consecutive two months, but it fell dramatically to 2.6% in June. The Industrial value added of Liaoning Province suffered a negative growth with obvious fluctuations, which went down to 6.1% in March, to 9.8% in April by 3.7 percentage points, to 7.1% in May and to 7.8% in June. Heilongjiang's Industrial value added bounced back and surpassed Jilin's, respectively growing 0.8, 1.2, 2.1 and 5.0% on a year-on-year in each month from March to June basis and thus presenting an increasing uptrend (Figs. 1.3 and 1.4).

The industrial growth rates of Beijing, Tianjin and Hebei Province presented a differentiation trend. The growth rate of Tianjin's Industrial value added slowed down from 9.2% early this year to 8.9% in June. The industrial value added of Hebei and Beijing ascended slowly from 4.2 and −2.5% early this year to 5.1 and 1.7% respectively in June (as illustrated in Fig. 1.5). In the first half of 2016, the industrial value added of Beijing, Tianjin and Hebei Province grew year on year by −1.0, −0.5 and 0.6 percentage point respectively as against the same period last year (Table 1.3).

Despite the slowdown of industrial investment growth rate, the investment structure was optimized. In the first half of 2016, the fixed asset investment in industry amounted to 9959.4 billion yuan, growing 4.2% year on year and descending 2.5 percentage points as against the first quarter. The fixed asset investment in mining industry amounted to 422.5 billion yuan, descending 19.7% year on year and rising by 1.6 percentage points over the first quarter. The fixed asset investment in manufacturing industry amounted to 8226.1 billion yuan,

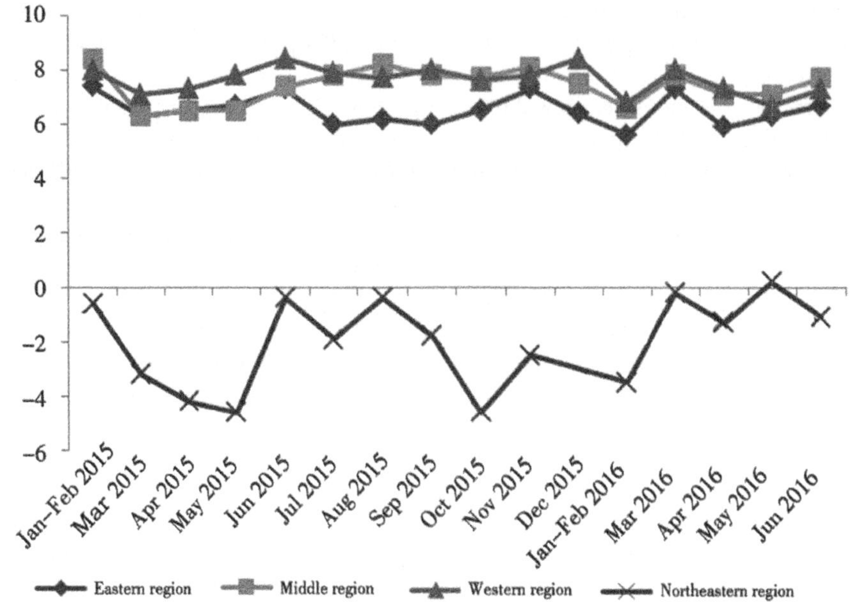

Fig. 1.3 Year-on-year growth rates of local industrial value added since 2015. *Source* National Bureau of Statistics website

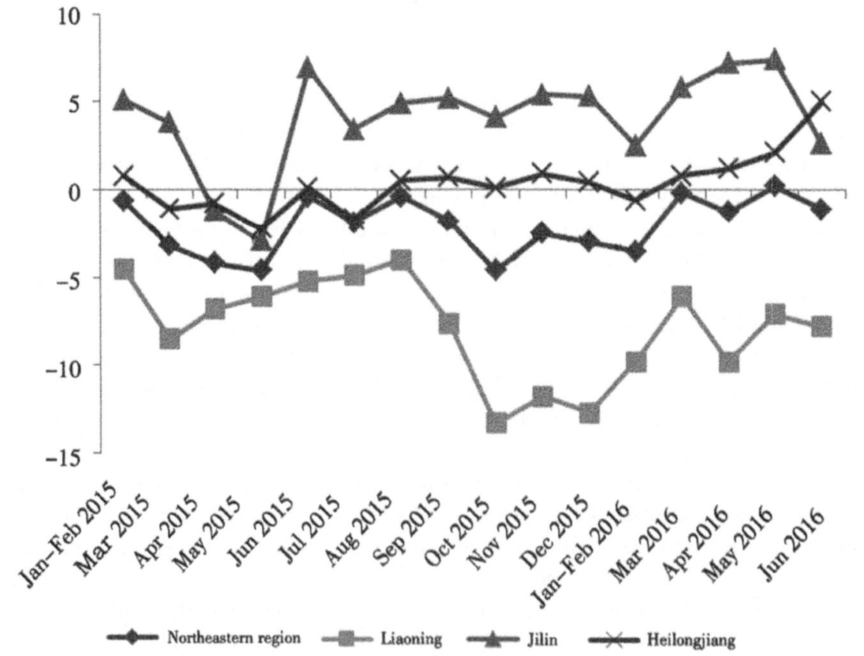

Fig. 1.4 Year-on-year growth rates of the industrial value added in three northeastern provinces since 2015. *Source* National Bureau of Statistics website

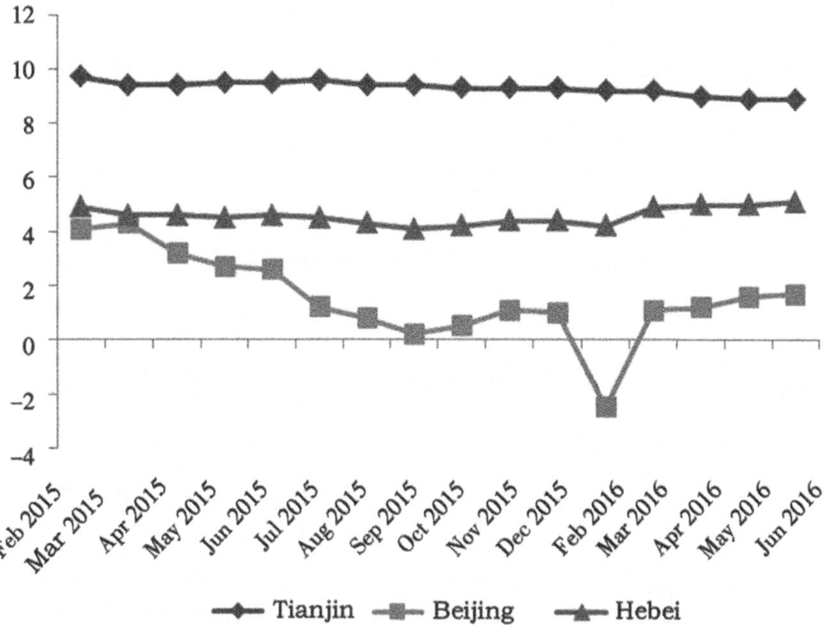

Fig. 1.5 Accumulative growth rates of the industrial value added in Beijing, Tianjin and Hebei Province since 2015. *Source* National Bureau of Statistics website

ascending 3.3% year on year and descending 3.1 percentage points as against the first quarter. The fixed asset investment in production and supply of electric power, heating power, fuel gas and water amounted to 1310.8 billion yuan, growing 22.5% year on year and rising by 3.1 percentage points over the first quarter. From January to May investment in industrial technical transformation grew 14.9%, 9.5 percentage points higher than the growth rate of total industrial investment, and the investment in technical transformation of manufacturing industry grew 15.2%, 10.6 percentage points higher than the growth rate of total investment in manufacturing industry. From January to May, investment in hi-tech industries grew 13.6%, 4 percentage points higher than the growth rate of total investment. There was a declining amount of investment in highly energy-consuming industries. From January to May, the fixed asset investment fell 4.6, 4.2 and 0.5% respectively in the petroleum refining and coking and nuclear fuel processing industry, the chemical raw materials and chemical products manufacturing industry and the non-metal mineral products manufacturing industry (Fig. 1.6).

The decreasing amplitude of industrial export continued to narrow. In the first half of 2016, industrial enterprises above a designated scale realized an export delivery value of 5511.7 billion yuan, with a year-on-year decline of 0.7%, narrowing 1.1 percentage points as against the whole year of 2015 and 2.3 percentage points as against the first quarter of this year. In June, industrial enterprises realized

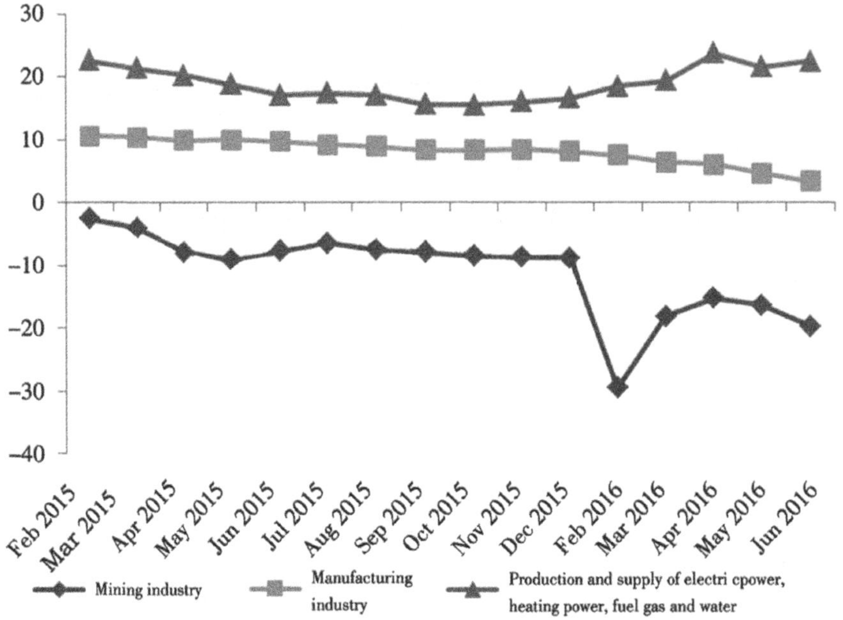

Fig. 1.6 Accumulative growth rates of fixed asset investment in three major industrial categories since 2015. *Source* National Bureau of Statistics website

an export delivery value of 1049.1 billion yuan, with a nominal year-on-year growth rate of 2.3%, presenting a positive growth for two consecutive years (Fig. 1.7).

The industrial enterprises' profits continued the growing trend, and the industrial profits of such main raw materials as coal, steel and non-ferrous metal continued the trend of recovery growth. From January to May, the total profit realized by industrial enterprises above a designated scale throughout China amounted to 2381.64 billion yuan, with a year-on-year growth rate of 6.4%, 8.7 percentage points higher than the year of 2015 but 1.0 percentage point lower than the first quarter of 2016. From January to May the mining industry suffered a loss of 5.41 billion yuan, with a year-on-year decline of 108.5%, 35.6 percentage points higher than the year of 2015 but 14.7% percentage points lower than the first quarter of 2016; the total profits realized by manufacturing industry amounted to 2163.26 billion yuan, with a year-on-year growth rate of 12.5, 9.7% percentage points higher than the year of 2015 but 2.1 percentage points lower than the first quarter of 2016; the total profits realized by production and supply of electric power, heating power, fuel gas and water amounted to 211.72 billion yuan, with a year-on-year growth rate of 1.3%, 12.2 percentage points lower than the year of 2015 and 3.3 percentage points than the first quarter of 2016. The industrial profits of such main raw materials as coal, steel and non-ferrous metal continued the trend of recovery growth. In May, the coal mining, ferrous metal smelting and rolling

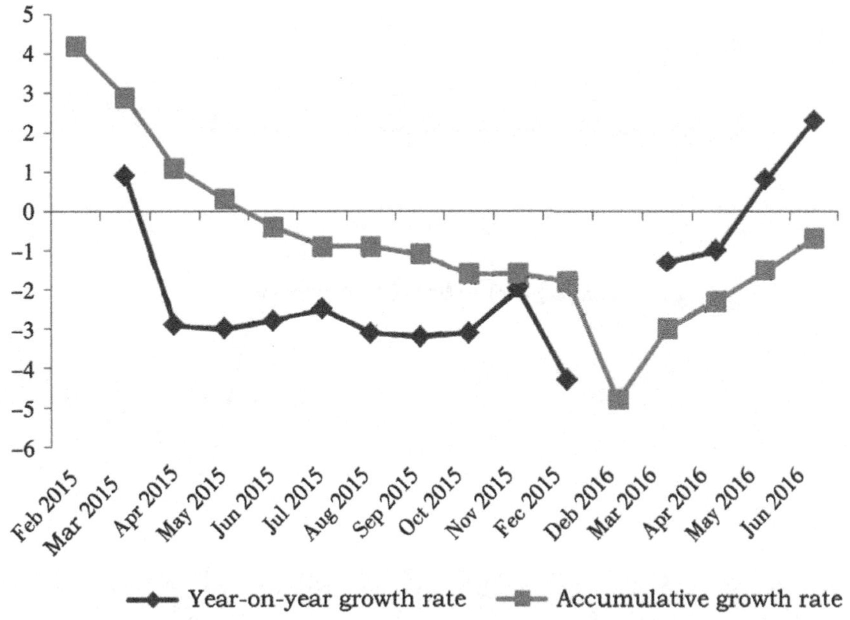

Fig. 1.7 Year-on-year and accumulative growth rates of industrial export delivery value since 2015. *Source* National Bureau of Statistics website

processing and non-ferrous metal smelting and rolling processing industries earned profit growth rates of 2.5-fold, 1.6-fold and 32.1% respectively (Fig. 1.8).

The decreasing amplitude of industrial products' ex-factory prices continued to narrow and enterprise's inventory pressure was slightly eased. The industrial products' ex-factory prices fell 2.6% year on year in June 2016, narrowing for six consecutive months. At the end of May, the industrial enterprises' manufactured inventory fell 1.1% year on year, declining for two consecutive months, and there were 14.9 days of the manufactured inventory turnover, shortened by 0.5 day year on year (Fig. 1.9).

There was still a long way to go to de-capacity. In March, April, May and June 2016, China's crude steel output grew 2.9, 0.5, 1.8 and 1.7% respectively, putting an end to the trend of persistent negative growth since October 2014. In the first half of 2016, Hebei, Jiangsu and Shandong produced 99.896 million tons, 55.609 million tons and 34.764 million tons of crude steel respectively, higher than 98.895 million tons, 54.019 million tons and 33.263 million tons in the same period last year and rising by 1.0, 2.9 and 4.5% respectively over the same period last year. As a matter of fact, a round of strong rebounds in steel price and the rising profit of steel industry since February 2016 had resumed large-scale production even in some "zombie" steel works that suspended production but were not yet closed

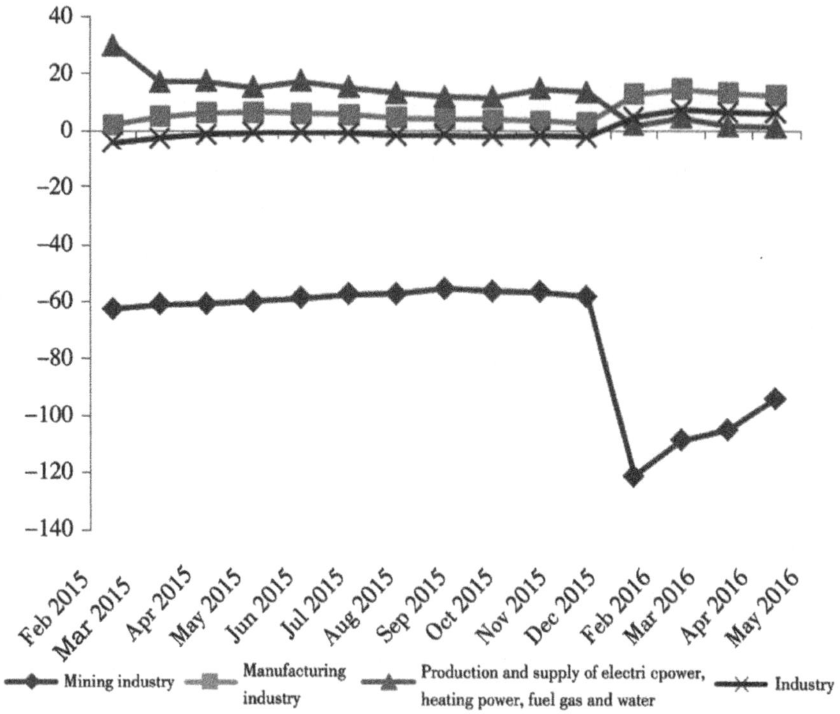

Fig. 1.8 Accumulative growth rates of three major industrial categories since 2015. *Source* National Bureau of Statistics website

down. China's average daily crude steel output hit a record high in April 2016, and the operating rate of blast furnaces in a hundred small- and medium-sized steel enterprises maintained above 85% in May. The resumed production of steel works added much difficulty to de-capacity task of the steel industry (Fig. 1.10).

1.2 Analysis of Industrial Operation

In the report, industries are classified by reference to criteria prescribed by the Ministry of Industry and Information Technology of the People's Republic of China into four major categories: raw materials industry, equipment industry, consumer goods industry as well as communication and electronic information and software industry. This report will focus on raw materials industry, equipment industry and consumer goods industry. The raw materials industry comprises energy sources, chemical, steel, non-ferrous metal and building materials. The equipment industry comprises machinery, automobile and civil ships. The consumer goods industry comprises light industry, textile, food and pharmaceutical.

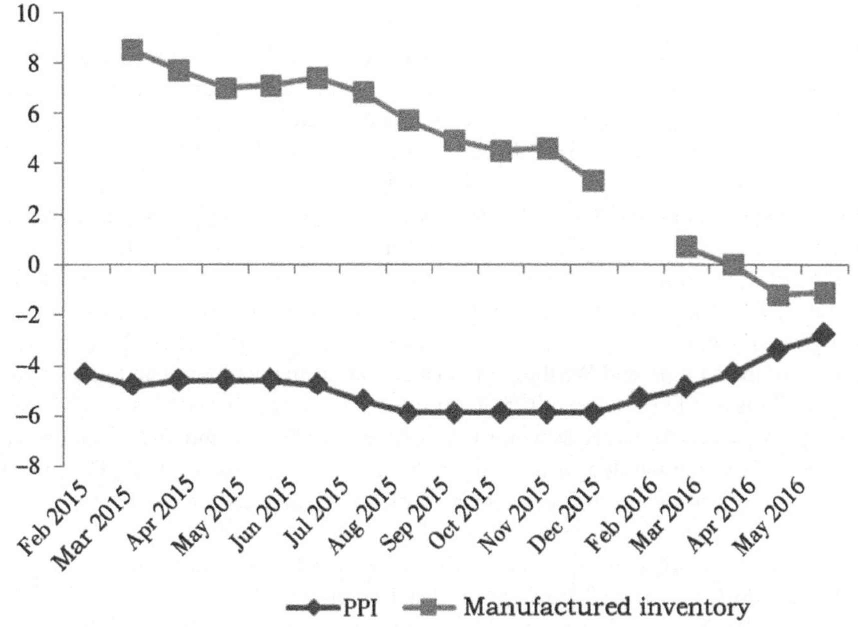

Fig. 1.9 Growth rates of PPI and manufactured inventory since 2015. *Source* National Bureau of Statistics website

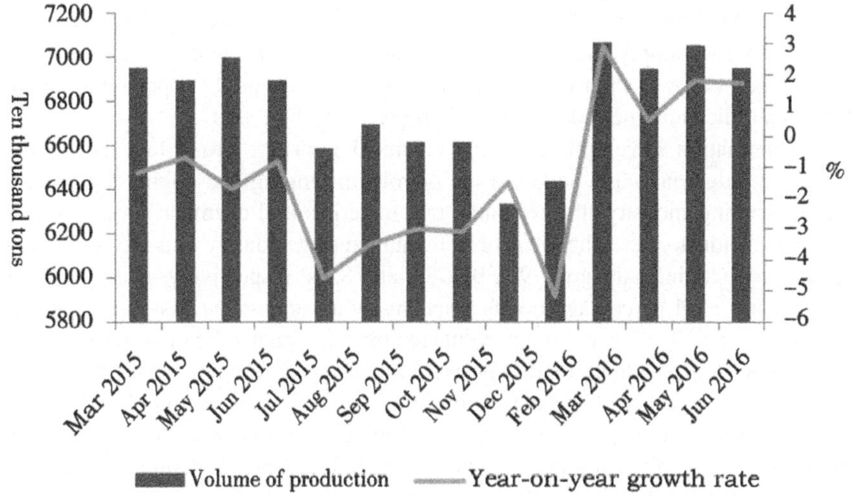

Fig. 1.10 Monthly outputs and year-on-year growth rates of crude steel since 2015. *Source* National Bureau of Statistics website

(1) **Raw materials industry**

The energy sources industry was under continuous adjustment. With contraction of market demands and change of energy supply-demand structure, the Mining and Washing of Coal as well as the petroleum and natural gas mining industry were subject to in-depth adjustment. From January to May 2016, the Industrial value added of Mining and Washing of Coal fell 1.4% year on year, 1.3 percentage points higher than the first quarter of this year and 3.3 percentage points higher than the growth rate in the whole of 2015. From January to May 2016, the Industrial value added of petroleum and natural gas mining industry grew 2.6%, 2.5 percentage points lower than the first quarter of this year and 1.6 percentage points lower than the growth rate in the whole year of 2015. From January to May 2016, the industrial profits of the Mining and Washing of Coal as well as the petroleum and natural gas mining industry fell 73.4 and 175.8% respectively, narrowing 19.2 and 26.2 percentage points respectively as against the first quarter but 8.4 and 101.3 percentage points higher than the decreasing amplitude in the whole year of 2015. Thus there seems no optimistic earning performance for the Mining and Washing of Coal as well as the petroleum and natural gas mining industry. From January to May 2016, exports of the Mining and Washing of Coal as well as the petroleum and natural gas mining industry continued the trend of negative growth.

Under the pressure of economic downturn, the electricity demand of the whole society may continue at a low level. From January to May 2016, the Industrial value added of the electric power and heating power production and supply industry grew 1.2% year on year, 0.1 percentage point lower than the first quarter of this year and 0.7 percentage points higher than the growth rate in the whole year of 2015. From January to May 2016, the industrial profits of the electric power and heating power production and supply industry fell 0.1% accumulatively year on year, 3.6 percentage points lower than the first quarter of this year and 13.9 percentage point lower than the same period last year (Table 1.1 and Fig. 1.11).

Differentiation development inside chemical industry: From January to May 2016, the industrial value added of the petroleum refining and coking and nuclear fuel processing industry, the chemical raw materials and chemical products manufacturing industry, the chemical fiber manufacturing industry and the rubber and plastic products industry grew 9.2, 9.5, 8.1 and 8.3% respectively, rising by −1.3, 0.7, 1.6 and −0.4 percentage points respectively as against the first quarter of this year and by 1.8, 0, −3.1 and 0.4 percentage points as against the growth rates in the whole year of 2015. On a monthly basis, in January and February and in March, the Industrial value added of the petroleum refining and coking and nuclear fuel processing industry grew 11.2 and 10.5% year on year respectively; the chemical raw materials and chemical products manufacturing industry grew 8.6 and 8.8% year on year respectively; the chemical fiber manufacturing industry grew 5.4 and 6.5% year on year respectively; and the rubber and plastic products industry grew 9.0 and 8.7% year on year respectively.

Benefiting from adjustment of lower oil price in previous period and of refined oil product pricing mechanism, in the period from January to May the industrial

Table 1.1 Accumulative growth rates of main indicators of the mining and washing of coal as well as the petroleum and natural gas mining industry (*Unit* %)

	Mining and washing of coal				Petroleum and natural gas mining industry			
	Revenue	Profit	Value of export delivery	Industrial value added	Revenue	Profit	Value of export delivery	Industrial value added
2015-02	−8.3	−62.6	−58.3	3.6	−34.0	−74.9	−3.9	2.5
2015-03	−10.8	−61.9	−70.0	0.9	−34.3	−71.7	−10.3	4.7
2015-04	−13.0	−61.6	−61.2	0.9	−34.0	−71.7	−10.5	5.3
2015-05	−13.6	−66.8	−49.9	0.9	−33.2	−69.5	−15.9	5.7
2015-06	−13.0	−67.0	−48.8	0.6	−32.4	−68.4	−21.1	5.7
2015-07	−13.2	−66.0	−50.8	1.7	−31.8	−66.6	−22.3	5.4
2015-08	−13.9	−64.9	−21.3	2.0	−31.8	−67.3	−27.5	5.1
2015-09	−14.4	−64.4	−3.4	1.9	−32.2	−66.1	−30.2	4.7
2015-10	−14.6	−62.1	−30.8	1.8	−32.5	−68.6	−27.8	4.3
2015-11	−14.6	−61.2	−53.7	1.9	−32.7	−70.4	−32.7	4.0
2015-12	−14.8	−65.0	−46.1	1.9	−32.6	−74.5	−34.9	4.2
2016-02	−17.1	−111.1	6.3	−1.3	−31.8	−234.1	−60.5	5.0
2016-03	−15.8	−92.6	−20.0	−0.1	−30.9	−202.0	−52.3	5.1
2016-04	−14.8	−92.2	−26.2	−0.5	−29.0	−196.0	−71.4	3.7
2016-05	−13.5	−73.4	25.5	−1.4	−27.2	−175.8	−68.1	2.6

Source National Bureau of Statistics website

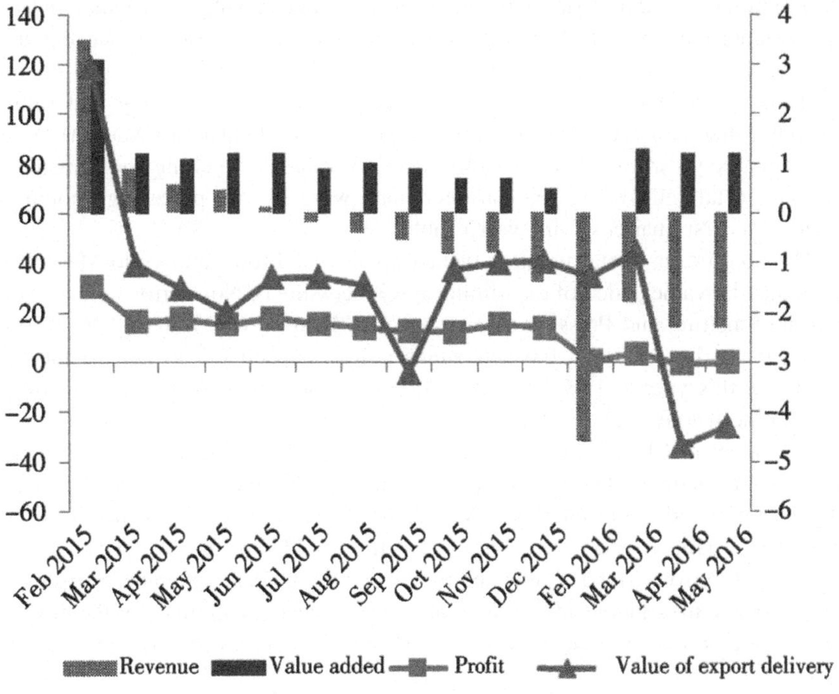

Fig. 1.11 Accumulative growth rates of main indicators of the electric power and heating power production and supply industry (*Unit* %). *Source* National Bureau of Statistics website

profit of the petroleum refining and coking and nuclear fuel processing industry tripled; the chemical raw materials and chemical products manufacturing industry earned a profit of 183.26 billion yuan, growing 14.7% year on year; the rubber and plastic products industry earned a year-on-year profit growth rate of 12.4%, 8.1 percentage points higher than the same period last year; however, the chemical fiber manufacturing industry reversed with a declining year-on-year profit growth rate of 7.5%, 64.2 percentage points down from the same period last year (Table 1.2).

The steel industry operated at a low level. From January to May 2016, the industrial value added of the Mining and Processing of Ferrous Metals Ores and the Smelting and Pressing of Ferrous Metal grew 1.8 and 1.5% respectively, falling by 0.4 and 2.2 percentage points as against the first quarter of this year and by 0.7 and 3.9 percentage points as against the growth rates in the whole year of 2015.

The steel industry's earning performance improved greatly. From January to May 2016, the decreasing amplitudes of revenues and profits of the Mining and Processing of Ferrous Metals Ores narrowed by 10.4 and 36.7 percentage points respectively as against the same period last year and by 4.8 and 4.4 percentage points respectively as against the first quarter of this year. From January to May this year, the decreasing amplitudes of the revenues of Smelting and Pressing of Ferrous Metal and profits narrowed by 2.7 and 86.3 percentage points as against the same period last year. The decreasing amplitude of the revenues of Smelting and Pressing of Ferrous Metal narrowed by 3.2 percentage points as against the first quarter, but the industry's profit growth rate realized a positive growth in April. Under the background of excess capacity and slowing fixed asset investment in the whole steel industry, a round of strong rebounds in steel price recently contributed most to greatly improving the steel industry's performance. As a matter of fact, the steel price began a round of rebounds in December 2015 and the prices of part of steel products bounced over 50%. The export of ferrous metal smelting and rolling continued the downtrend of the previous year. From January to May 2016, the accumulative growth rates of the export delivery value of Smelting and Pressing of Ferrous Metal fell 18.6% year on year, narrowing by 5.2 percentage points as against the first quarter of this year (Table 1.3).

The non-ferrous metal industry picked up slowly. From January to May 2016, the industrial value added of the Mining and Processing of Non-ferrous Metals Ores and the Smelting and Pressing of Non-ferrous Metal grew 5.9 and 10.3% respectively, rising by −1.7 and 0.6 percentage points respectively as against the first quarter of this year and by 1.6 and −1.0 percentage points as against the growth rates in the whole year of 2015.

The prices of China's main non-ferrous metal products fluctuated at a low level and went up slowly. The earning performance of the non-ferrous metal industry slightly improved. From January to May 2016, the accumulative growth rates of the revenues of Mining and Processing of Non-ferrous Metals Ores and Smelting and Pressing of Ferrous Metal accelerated by 1.8 and 0.3 percentage points respectively as against the first quarter of this year, and the decreasing amplitude of the profit of Mining and Processing of Non-ferrous Metals Ores narrowed by 1.8 and 15.0

Table 1.2 Accumulative growth rates of the chemical industry's main indicators (*Unit %*)

	Petroleum refining and coking and nuclear fuel processing industry				Chemical raw materials and chemical products manufacturing industry			
	Revenue	Profit	Value of export delivery	Industrial value added	Revenue	Profit	Value of export delivery	Industrial value added
Feb 2015	−22.2	−345.3	−42.0	3.5	2.9	1.2	−1.6	9.4
Mar 2015	−19.7	−239.9	−39.3	5.4	2.7	6.0	0.5	9.5
Apr 2015	−17.8	−99.9	−35.2	6.8	3.1	10.5	−0.7	9.8
May 2015	−16.5	67.0	−29.6	7.6	3.0	12.6	−1.9	9.6
Jun 2015	−16.3	78.7	−25.1	7.8	3.2	13.0	−3.6	9.6
July 2015	−16.1	81.5	−26.8	7.8	3.2	13.5	−2.9	9.5
Aug 2015	−16.6	50.5	−25.0	7.8	3.7	12.2	−3.6	9.6
Sep 2015	−17.2	53.5	−21.3	7.6	3.3	10.1	−4.2	9.6
Oct 2015	−17.3	76.1	−17.0	7.5	2.8	8.6	−4.8	9.6
Nov 2015	−16.8	138.8	−14.8	7.6	2.6	8.3	−4.4	9.5
Dec 2015	−16.3	966.8	−10.3	7.4	2.3	7.7	−4.2	9.5
Feb 2016	−4.6	−185.7	33.1	11.2	2.5	16.2	−0.5	8.6
Mar 2016	−4.5	Lost last year	27.7	10.5	3.8	20.8	−1.1	8.8
Apr 2016	−6.7	8204.8	18.9	10.1	3.6	18.3	−1.5	9.1
May 2016	−7.6	303.9	15.0	9.2	4.2	14.7	3.4	9.5
	Chemical fiber manufacturing industry				Rubber and plastic products industry			
	Revenue	Profit	Value of export delivery	Industrial value added	Revenue	Profit	Value of export delivery	Industrial value added
Feb 2015	2.4	31.8	−10.7	9.5	6.9	6.4	−0.9	8.7
Mar 2015	1.3	44.6	−11.3	10.1	**5.0**	3.5	−4.1	8.3
Apr 2015	2.1	54.4	−10.4	11.1	4.4	4.6	−4.3	8.0
May 2015	3.1	56.7	−10.2	11.9	4.5	4.3	−5.6	8.1

(continued)

Table 1.2 (continued)

	Chemical fiber manufacturing industry				Rubber and plastic products industry			
	Revenue	Profit	Value of export delivery	Industrial value added	Revenue	Profit	Value of export delivery	Industrial value added
Jun 2015	2.8	50.6	−8.9	12.0	5.3	5.1	−5.7	8.3
July 2015	2.7	42.3	−8.1	11.4	5.2	6.0	−5.5	8.6
Aug 2015	1.7	39.3	−8.0	11.0	5.7	6.3	−5.7	8.8
Sep 2015	1.2	35.1	−8.7	11.1	5.5	6.8	−5.9	8.8
Oct 2015	0.7	30.4	−8.7	11.1	4.9	6.5	−6.3	8.6
Nov 2015	1.0	24.1	−9.1	11.2	4.5	5.4	−6.2	8.2
Dec 2015	1.2	15.2	−8.8	11.2	4.1	4.6	−6.2	7.9
Feb 2016	−2.6	−4.0	7.6	5.4	4.1	11.0	1.9	9.0
Mar 2016	0.5	1.8	7.9	6.5	5.9	13.6	4.3	8.7
Apr 2016	0.5	−5.0	6.8	7.2	5.0	12.8	2.4	8.4
May 2016	1.0	−7.5	8.6	8.1	5.2	12.4	3.2	8.3

Source National Bureau of Statistics website

Table 1.3 Accumulative growth rates of the steel industry's main indicators (*Unit %*)

	Mining and processing of ferrous metals ores				Smelting and pressing of ferrous metal			
	Revenue	Profit	Value of export delivery	Industrial value added	Revenue	Profit	Value of export delivery	Industrial value added
Feb 2015	−17.5	−43.5	−100.0	10.4	−10.4	−10.8	14.3	3.5
Mar 2015	−20.2	−49.3		7.5	−9.7	2.2	6.3	4.2
Apr 2015	−20.9	−49.6		6.4	−9.8	−2.7	−0.9	4.7
May 2015	−20.3	−46.7		6.5	−10.2	−11.5	−5.0	4.9
Jun 2015	−20.2	−47.5		6.0	−10.4	−22.5	−8.6	5.2
July 2015	−19.6	−45.5		6.2	−11.0	−38.0	−15.9	5.0
Aug 2015	−19.2	−44.4		6.0	−11.7	−51.6	−11.8	5.1
Sep 2015	−19.4	−42.3		5.4	−12.2	−60.5	−12.1	5.2
Oct 2015	−19.8	−43.2		4.5	−12.6	−68.3	−13.7	5.2
Nov 2015	−20.1	−42.4		3.5	−12.5	−68.0	−15.5	5.4
Dec 2015	−20.7	−43.9		2.5	−13.0	−67.9	−15.1	5.4
Feb 2016	−18.5	−18.5		0.3	−13.2	−72.9	−25.8	4.0
Mar 2016	−14.7	−14.4	−90.0	2.2	−10.7	−15.8	−23.8	3.7
Apr 2016	−12.6	−9.4	−94.1	2.4	−9.4	41.9	−19.5	2.5
May 2016	−9.9	−10.0	−94.4	1.8	−7.5	74.8	−18.6	1.5

Source National Bureau of Statistics website

percentage points as against the same period last year and the first quarter of this year respectively.

In April 2016, the growth rate of the profit of Smelting and Pressing of Non-ferrous Metal realized the transition from a negative to a positive; and from January to May, the profit of Smelting and Pressing of Non-ferrous Metal grew 13.4% year on year. From January to May 2016, the export of Mining and Processing of Non-ferrous Metals Ores was better than that of Smelting and Pressing of Non-ferrous Metal; the export delivery value of Mining and Processing of Non-ferrous Metals Ores grew 58.3% year on year while the Smelting and Pressing of Non-ferrous Metal remained at a negative growth. From January to May, the export delivery value of Smelting and Pressing of Non-ferrous Metal fell 10.0% year on year, with the decreasing amplitude narrowing by 8.2 percentage points as against the first quarter (Table 1.4).

The building materials industry recovered slightly. Driven by a favorable turn in the real estate industry, the building materials industry presented a slight uptrend. From January to May 2016, the industrial value added of the non-metal minerals mining and dressing industry, the wood processing and wood, bamboo, rattan, palm and straw-made products industry and the non-metal mineral products industry grew 5.8, 6.1 and 8.1% year on year respectively, rising by 0.1, 0.1 and 0.5 percentage points respectively as against the first quarter of this year; and the Industrial value added of the non-metal mineral products industry went up by 1.6 percentage points as against the growth rate in the whole year of 2015.

From January to May 2016, the industrial revenues of the non-metal minerals mining and dressing industry, the wood processing and wood, bamboo, rattan, palm and straw-made products industry and the non-metal mineral products industry grew 5.4, 6.5 and 4.7% respectively, rising by 1.4, 0.9 and 1.1 percentage points respectively as against the first quarter of this year; the three industries' profits grew 4.6, 8.7 and 4.1% respectively, rising by 0.5, 0.8 and 4.3 percentage points as against the first quarter of this year. From January to May 2016, in terms of the building materials industry's export, the non-metal mineral products industry continued last year's downtrend while the non-metal minerals mining and dressing industry and the wood processing and wood, bamboo, rattan, palm and straw-made products industry achieved 11.1 and 9.5% growth rates of export delivery value respectively (Table 1.5 and Fig. 1.12).

(2) **Equipment manufacturing industry**

The machinery industry stabilized at a low level. From January to May 2016, the industrial value added of the metal products industry, the general-purpose equipment manufacturing industry, the special-purpose equipment manufacturing industry, the railway, ship, aerospace and other transport equipment manufacturing industry, the electric machinery and equipment manufacturing industry, the instrument and apparatus manufacturing industry, and the metal products, machinery and equipment repairing industry grew 8.6, 4.4, 4.5, 4.5, 8.7, 7.3 and 15.7% respectively, rising by 0.3, −0.4, 0.7, 0.1, 0.0, 0.6 and −1.6 percentage

Table 1.4 Accumulative growth rates of main indicators of non-ferrous metal industry (*Unit %*)

	Mining and processing of non-ferrous metals ores				Smelting and pressing of non-ferrous metal			
	Revenue	Profit	Value of export delivery	Industrial value added	Revenue	Profit	Value of export delivery	Industrial value added
Feb 2015	2.2	−16.3	−32.5	4.7	1.2	12.6	−0.2	12.7
Mar 2015	−1.0	−22.9	−16.7	2.2	1.6	28.2	−1.1	11.5
Apr 2015	−1.2	−21.8	−16.7	1.8	1.9	32.4	−0.3	10.6
May 2015	−1.8	−19.9	−12.6	2.2	2.8	28.2	−4.9	10.2
Jun 2015	−0.9	−17.4	17.2	2.8	2.5	18.1	−3.8	10.5
July 2015	−0.7	−20.1	−17.5	3.3	2.4	11.3	−7.0	10.9
Aug 2015	−0.2	−19.9	−8.2	3.9	2.5	3.6	−8.8	11.0
Sep 2015	0.2	−20.3	−6.0	4.1	2.6	−1.9	−10.1	11.1
Oct 2015	−0.7	−19.7	1.8	4.1	2.1	−4.8	−13.7	11.2
Nov 2015	−1.6	−19.8	−6.4	4.0	1.1	−6.9	−12.8	11.3
Dec 2015	−2.5	−19.3	−23.0	4.3	0.7	−11.0	−10.8	11.3
Feb 2016	−0.5	−11.4	250.0	8.3	−0.9	−12.9	−27.1	10.2
Mar 2016	1.4	−6.7	55.6	7.6	2. 2	−4.3	−18.2	9.7
Apr 2016	2.3	−8.1	−11.1	6. 7	2. 6	6.6	−12.7	10.1
May 2016	3.2	−4.9	58.3	5. 9	2. 5	13.4	−10.0	10.3

Source National Bureau of Statistics website

Table 1.5 Accumulative growth rates of main indicators of the non-metal minerals mining and dressing industry and the non-metal mineral products industry (*Unit* %)

	Non-metal minerals mining and dressing industry				Non-metal mineral products industry			
	Revenue	Profit	Value of export delivery	Industrial value added	Revenue	Profit	Value of export delivery	Industrial value added
Feb 2015	7.8	7.3	5.6	9.2	9.5	3.1	−2.3	10.4
Mar 2015	6.1	4.6	−19.1	8.2	5.8	0.1	−2.9	7.6
Apr 2015	4.8	4.0	−44.0	8.0	4.3	−4.4	−4.5	6.6
May 2015	4.6	4.4	−39.8	7.5	3.6	−6.4	−4.4	6.3
Jun 2015	4.8	4.6	−40.2	7.4	3.7	−6.7	−4.7	6.4
July 2015	4.7	5.0	−31.6	7.5	3.6	−7.7	−4.2	6.4
Aug 2015	5.1	5.0	−30.7	7.7	3.7	−8.0	−3.3	6.6
Sep 2015	5.3	5.8	−39.9	7.6	3.7	−8.1	−3.2	6.8
Oct 2015	5.0	6.1	−38.8	7.3	3.2	−8.2	−4.8	6.6
Nov 2015	4.4	5.2	−35.7	6.9	3.0	−8.8	−4.2	6.5
Dec 2015	3.7	4.9	−38.6	6.6	2.8	−9.0	−4.3	6.5
Feb 2016	4.3	2.4	−50.0	5.3	1.4	−3.8	−4.1	6.0
Mar 2016	4.0	4.1	−27.8	5.7	3.6	−0.2	−3.4	7.6
Apr 2016	3.9	1.9	3.8	5. 8	4.0	0.9	−3.1	8.1
May 2016	5.4	4.6	11.1	5.8	4.7	4.1	−3.2	8.1

Source National Bureau of Statistics website

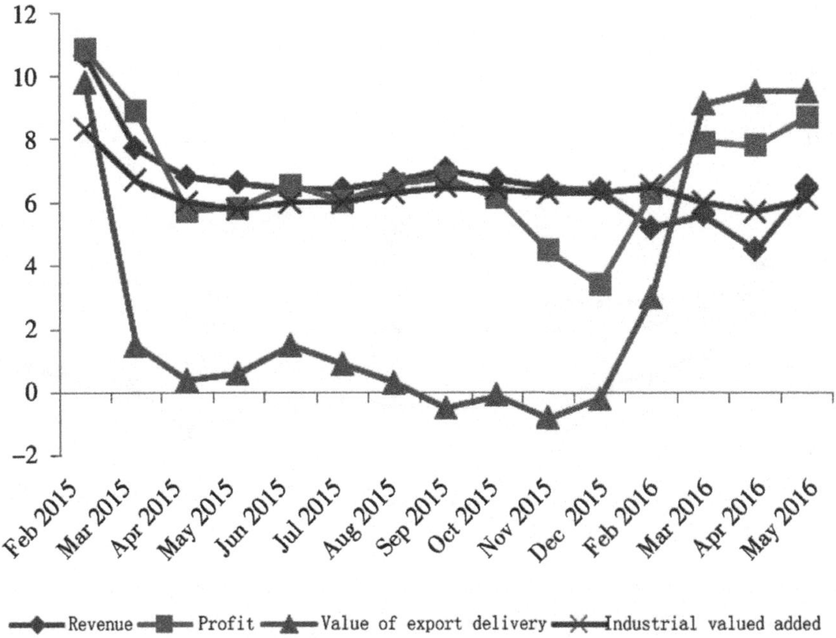

Fig. 1.12 Accumulative growth rates of main indicators of the wood processing and wood, bamboo, rattan, palm and straw-made products industry. *Source* National Bureau of Statistics website

points respectively as against the first quarter of this year and by 1.2, 1.5, 1.1, −2.3, 1.4, 1.9 and 6.9 percentage points respectively as against the growth rates in the whole year of 2015.

The machinery industry's profits began picking up. From January to May 2016, thanks to upgrading of part of enterprises' products and rapid development of intelligent products, the electric machinery and apparatus manufacturing industry presented a remarkable earning performance (as illustrated in Fig. 1.13), and its revenue and profit accumulatively grew 7.6 and 18.4% respectively, rising by 0.8 and 0.4 percentage points respectively as against the first quarter of this year and by 2.9 and 12.9 percentage points respectively as against the same period last year. The metal products, machinery and equipment repairing industry's revenue and profit accumulatively grew 17.6 and 21.5% respectively, falling by 3.4 and 9.1 percentage points respectively as against the first quarter of this year but rising by 24.4 and 16.2 percentage points respectively as against the same period last year. From January to May, the general-purpose equipment manufacturing industry, the special-purpose equipment manufacturing industry, the railway, ship, aerospace and other transport equipment manufacturing industry, the instrument and apparatus manufacturing industry, and the metal products industry achieved accumulative year-on-year growth rates of 2.6, 5.2, 2.4, 7.0 and 4.7% respectively in their

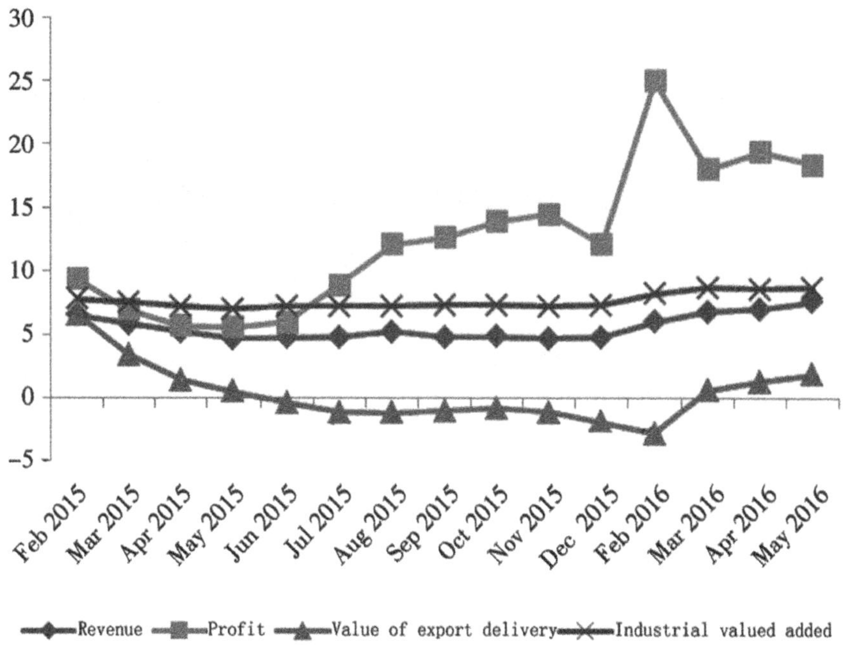

Fig. 1.13 Accumulative growth rates of the electric machinery and equipment manufacturing industry's main indicators (*Unit %*). *Source* National Bureau of Statistics website

industrial revenues, rising by 0.8, −0.6, 0.6, 0.7 and 1.3 percentage points as against the first quarter of this year, and also achieved accumulative year-on-year growth rates of 2.0, 2.3, 6.1, 8.4 and 9.5% respectively in their industrial profits, rising by 0.7, −6.1, 6.0, 0.7 and 3.3 percentage points respectively as against the first quarter of this year.

The machinery industry's export situation seemed less optimistic. From January to May 2016, the general-purpose equipment manufacturing industry, the railway, ship, aerospace and other transport equipment manufacturing industry, and the metal products industry suffered a negative year-on-year growth rate of export delivery value, which fell 6.3, 4.6 and 5.9% respectively, exceeding the decreasing amplitude in the whole year of 2015 by 3.3, 1.4 and 3.3 percentage points respectively. The special-purpose equipment manufacturing industry and the instrument and apparatus manufacturing industry gained year-on-year growth rates of 0.7 and 3.1% in export delivery value respectively, and the growth rate of the special-purpose equipment manufacturing industry's export delivery value tended to slow down, declining from 3.8% in February to 0.7% in May (Table 1.6).

The automobile manufacturing industry continued growing. From January to May 2016, the Industrial value added of the automobile industry grew 10.4% year on year, 0.9 percentage point higher than the first quarter of this year and 3.7 percentage points higher than the growth rates in the whole year of 2015. In April

Table 1.6 Accumulative growth rates of the machinery industry's main indicators (*Unit %*)

	General-purpose equipment manufacturing industry				Special-purpose equipment manufacturing industry			
	Revenue	Profit	Value of export delivery	Industrial value added	Revenue	Profit	Value of export delivery	Industrial value added
Feb 2015	3.9	4.2	6.3	4.8	4.5	−1.1	1.1	3.1
Mar 2015	3.5	2.2	2.1	3.9	2.9	−1.7	4.6	1.8
Apr 2015	1.7	−1.1	0.3	3.6	2.3	−0.9	4.2	2.0
May 2015	1.3	−1.2	−0.7	3.4	2.3	−2.2	3.8	2.2
Jun 2015	1.5	−0.1	−1.6	3.5	2.8	−3.4	2.4	2.7
July 2015	1.4	1.2	−3.3	3.6	3.1	−2.6	0.5	3.0
Aug 2015	1.5	0.6	−3.6	3.6	3.5	−3.0	−1.4	3.3
Sep 2015	1.3	0.7	−4.3	3.4	3.3	−5.0	−2.7	3.4
Oct 2015	0.9	0.3	−4.7	3.2	3.4	−3.4	−2.7	3.5
Nov 2015	0.8	−0.7	−5.3	3.1	3.3	−4.0	−3.0	3.4
Dec 2015	0.3	−0.6	−4.9	2.9	2.9	−3.4	−3.0	3.4
Feb 2016	1.3	−1.1	−8.8	3.9	4.9	12.8	3.8	3.5
Mar 2016	1.8	1.3	−6.6	4.8	5.8	8.4	1.8	3.8
Apr 2016	1.7	0.7	−5.7	4.5	4.8	2.3	0.9	4.1
May 2016	2.6	2.0	−6.3	4.4	5.2	2.3	0.7	4.5
	Railway, ship, aerospace and other transport equipment manufacturing				Instrument and apparatus manufacturing			
	Revenue	Profit	Value of export delivery	Industrial value added	Revenue	Profit	Value of export delivery	Industrial value added
Feb 2015	13.6	31.5	8.5	10.5	9.5	7.5	11.4	7.4
Mar 2015	12.5	17.8	11.5	12.6	9.4	8.4	10.5	7.6
Apr 2015	11.4	14.2	11.5	11.7	8.3	2.6	8.5	7.3

(continued)

Table 1.6 (continued)

	Railway, ship, aerospace and other transport equipment manufacturing				Instrument and apparatus manufacturing			
	Revenue	Profit	Value of export delivery	Industrial value added	Revenue	Profit	Value of export delivery	Industrial value added
May 2015	9.3	9.0	9.5	10.3	7.8	2.8	7.4	6.5
Jun 2015	7.8	5.4	7.0	9.8	7.9	4.5	6.6	6.6
July 2015	7.4	2.3	6.3	9.5	7.3	4.7	5.8	6.4
Aug 2015	6.7	1.9	6.1	8.9	7.1	5.9	5.2	6.1
Sep 2015	6.1	3.6	4.9	8.4	6.9	4.7	4.6	5.9
Oct 2015	5.5	3.3	3.9	7.6	6.9	6.4	4.2	5.7
Nov 2015	5.5	4.2	3.0	7.1	6.4	4.9	3.8	5.3
Dec 2015	5.3	6.1	1.4	6.8	5.8	6.1	3.1	5.4
Feb 2016	2.4	2.5	1.8	5.2	4.7	4.9	−3.1	5.4
Mar 2016	1.8	0.1	1.2	4.4	6.3	7.7	1.7	6.7
Apr 2016	1.0	3.0	−3.4	4.2	5.8	7.2	2.8	6.7
May 2016	2.4	6.1	−4.6	4.5	7.0	8.4	3.1	7.3
	Metal products manufacturing				Metal products, machinery and equipment repairing industry			
	Revenue	Profit	Value of export delivery	Industrial value added	Revenue	Profit	Value of export delivery	Industrial value added
Feb 2015	10.8	19.2	8.5	9.7	−2.6	−2.9	24.3	8.2
Mar 2015	8.9	12.9	5.6	9.1	−4.1	−0.5	9.7	7.0
Apr 2015	7.1	11.4	3.9	8.6	−5.0	10.1	4.4	5.0
May 2015	6.1	9.8	1.6	8.3	−6.8	5.3	3.3	3.4
Jun 2015	6.3	10.4	0.9	8.3	−3.9	15.6	4.7	4.8
July 2015	6.1	9.9	−0.3	8.2	−1.4	23.0	3.4	6.2

(continued)

Table 1.6 (continued)

	Metal products manufacturing				Metal products, machinery and equipment repairing industry			
	Revenue	Profit	Value of export delivery	Industrial value added	Revenue	Profit	Value of export delivery	Industrial value added
Aug 2015	5.8	9.3	−1.7	7.9	1. 7	21.0	9.1	7.8
Sep 2015	5.4	8.9	−2.4	7.6	12.0	27.1	14.6	8.3
Oct 2015	5.1	8.2	−2.7	7.5	14.0	30.6	15.9	8.5
Nov 2015	4.7	6.5	−2.8	7.5	14.8	29.1	16.9	8.8
Dec 2015	4.5	4.7	−2.6	7.4	15.1	37.6	16.1	8.8
Feb 2016	2.6	4.4	−9.3	8.2	20.9	29.2	9.1	17.5
Mar 2016	3.4	6.2	−7.3	8.3	21.0	30.6	18.2	17.3
Apr 2016	3.6	6.8	−6.8	8.6	21.4	19.5	20.4	16.1
May 2016	4.7	9.5	−5.9	8.6	17.6	21.5	20.2	15.7

Source National Bureau of Statistics website

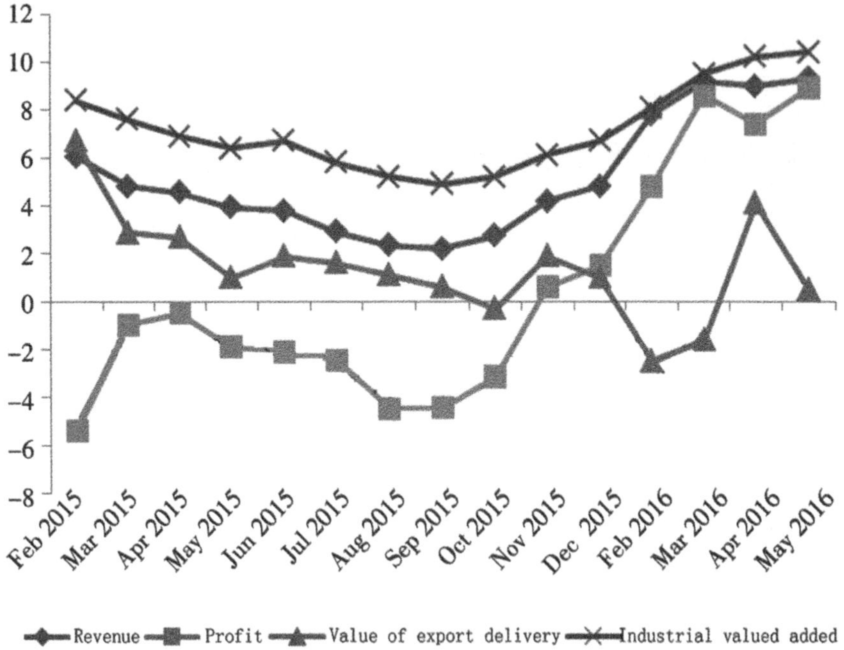

Fig. 1.14 Accumulative growth rates of the automobile industry's main indicators (*Unit* %). *Source* National Bureau of Statistics website

and May, the Industrial value added growth rate of the automobile industry exceeded 11% for two consecutive years (Fig. 1.14).

The earning performance of the automobile industry improved significantly. From January to May 2016, the automobile industry realized accumulative year-on-year growth rates of 9.3 and 8.9% respectively in its revenues and profits, rising by 0.1 and 0.4 percentage points respectively as against the first quarter of this year and by 4.5 and 7.4 percentage points respectively as against the growth rates in the whole year of 2015, which presented an obvious trend of recovery. Under the influence of such factors as sluggish peripheral markets, the export delivery value of the automobile industry accumulatively grew 0.5% year on year from January to May, increasing 2.1 percentage points over the first quarter of this year but decreasing 0.5 percentage points from the growth rates in the whole year of 2015.

(3) **Consumer goods industry**

The textile and wearing apparel industry remained sluggish. From January to May 2016, the industrial value added of the textile industry, the Manufacture of Textile, Wearing Apparel and Accessories as well as the leather, fur and feather products and shoemaking industry grew 7.4, 5.2 and 3.7% year on year respectively, rising by −0.3, 0 and 0.1 percentage points respectively as against the first quarter of this year and by 0.4, 0.8 and −1.2 percentage points as against the growth rates in the whole year of 2015.

The textile and wearing apparel industry was greeted with a slight pickup in its earnings growth rate. From January to May 2016, the total profits of the textile industry and the Manufacture of Textile, Wearing Apparel and Accessories grew 6.9 and 7.3% respectively, rising by 0.2 and 0.4 percentage points respectively over the first quarter of this year and by 1.8 and 3.3 percentage points as against the growth rates in the whole year of 2015. From January to May, the total profits of the leather, fur and feather products and shoemaking industry grew 4.9%, decreasing 2.4 percentage points as against the first quarter of this year.

The textile and wearing apparel industry first took a turn for the better. From January to May 2016, the export delivery values of the textile industry and the leather, fur and feather products and shoemaking industry grew 0.7 and 1.9% year on year respectively, rising by 0.5 and 1.3 percentage points respectively over the first quarter of this year; the Manufacture of Textile, Wearing Apparel and Accessories continued the negative growth trend in its export volume, but the decreasing amplitude tended to narrow (Table 1.7 and Fig. 1.15).

Differentiation of the food industry: From January to May 2016, the industrial value added of the farm and sideline food processing industry, the food manufacturing industry and the wine, beverage and refined tea manufacturing industry grew 6.2, 8.7 and 6.1% respectively year on year, 0.6, 0.1 and −1.1 percentage points higher as against the first quarter of this year respectively and rising by 0.7, 1.2 and −1.6 percentage points respectively as against the whole year of 2015. Since the beginning of this year, the growth rate of industrial value added of tobacco industry witnessed a sharp decline, but the decreasing amplitude tended to narrow on a monthly basis. From January to May, the value added of tobacco industry dropped 12.0% year on year, narrowing by 1.4 percentage points as against the first quarter of this year. In the first quarter of 2016, the drastic downsizing of cigarette production in China led to severe situation of commercial sales of tobacco products.

Profits dropped in tobacco industry and wine, beverage and refined tea manufacturing industries but improved markedly in farm and sideline food processing industry and food manufacturing industry. From January to May, the prime operating revenue and total profit of the farm and sideline food processing industry grew 5.7% and 11.7% year on year respectively, 0.6 and −0.4 percentage points respectively higher than the first quarter of this year and 2.2 and 5.3 percentage points respectively over the previous year; the prime operating revenue and total profit of the food manufacturing industry grew 7.8 and 15.1% year on year respectively, 0.3 and −2.4 percentage points higher than the first quarter of this year and 1.5 and 6.0 percentage points respectively higher than the previous year; the prime operating revenue and total profit of the wine, beverage and refined manufacturing industries grew 5.6 and 3.0% year on year respectively, 1.1 and 9.0 percentage points lower than the first quarter of this year and 0.8 and 4.5 percentage points lower than the previous year; and the prime operating revenue and total profit of the tobacco industry declined 11.7 and 24.0% year on year respectively, 0.6 and

Table 1.7 Accumulative growth rates of main indicators of the textile industry and the manufacture of textile, wearing apparel and accessories (*Unit %*)

	Textile industry				Manufacture of textile, wearing apparel and accessories			
	Revenue	Profit	Value of export delivery	Industrial value added	Revenue	Profit	Value of export delivery	Industrial value added
Feb 2015	6.4	8.9	0.2	7.2	8.1	10.4	−0.5	6.1
Mar 2015	5.1	6.8	−3.1	6.6	8.0	13.2	−0.1	6.1
Apr 2015	5.1	6.6	−4.2	6.6	7.2	8.2	−0.3	5.5
May 2015	5.1	6.3	−4.0	6.9	6.6	7.9	−0.9	5.3
Jun 2015	5.5	6.1	−3.6	7.1	6.2	7.3	−1.1	5.1
July 2015	5.7	7.0	−3.3	7.2	6.0	7.1	−0.9	4.9
Aug 2015	5.9	7.5	−3.2	7.3	6.0	6.3	−0.8	4.9
Sep 2015	5.7	7.8	−4.1	7.2	5.7	7.3	−1.0	4.7
Oct 2015	5.5	6.8	−4.5	7.0	5.5	5.6	−0.8	4.7
Nov 2015	5.3	5.9	−4.4	6.9	5.9	5.0	−0.6	4.5
Dec 2015	5.4	5.1	−3.9	7.0	5.6	4.0	−0.4	4.4
Feb 2016	5.0	7.0	−3.1	7.9	6.3	11.5	−1.0	5.3
Mar 2016	5.1	6.7	0.2	7.7	6.7	6.9	−0.6	5.2
Apr 2016	4.3	6.8	–	7.5	6.1	7.1	−0.2	5.3
May 2016	4.9	6.9	0.7	7.4	6.3	7.3	−0.2	5.2

Source National Bureau of Statistics website

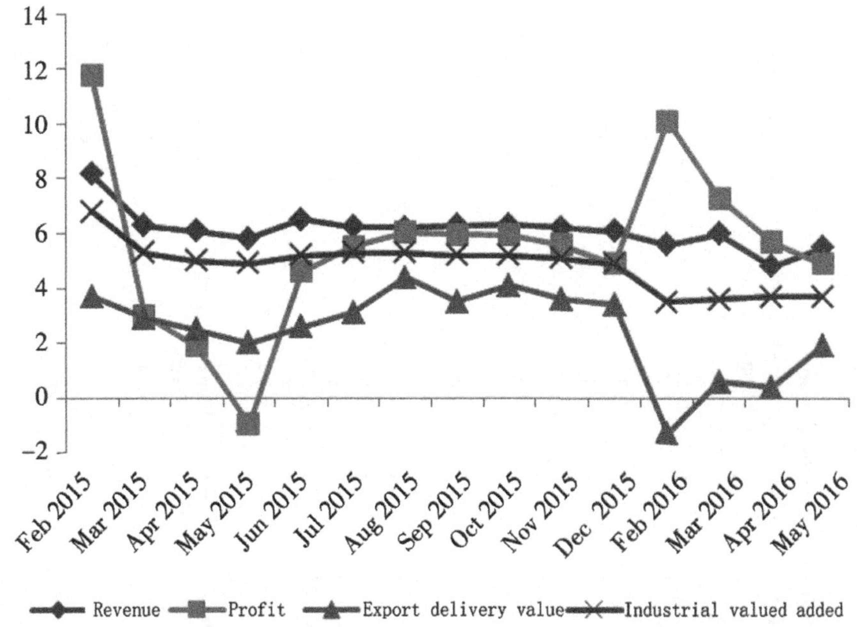

Fig. 1.15 Accumulative growth rates of main indicators of the leather, fur and feather products and shoemaking industry (*Unit* %). *Source* National Bureau of Statistics website

7.0 percentage point lower than the first quarter of this year and 17.2 and 22.6 percentage points lower than the previous year.

The export volume of the farm and sideline food processing industry and the food manufacturing industry turned for the better while the export growth rate of the tobacco industry and the wine, beverage and refined tea manufacturing industries just reversed. From January to May 2016, the export delivery value of the farm and sideline food processing industries and the food manufacturing industry grew 0.0% and 10.5% year on year respectively, 1.9 and 0.1 percentage point respectively higher than the first quarter of this year, and 6.8 and 9.4 percentage points respectively higher than the previous year; the export delivery value of the tobacco industry and the wine, beverage and refined tea manufacturing industries grew 6.1 and 9.0% year on year respectively, descending by 5.6 and 34.3 percentage points respectively from the first quarter of this year (Table 1.8).

The pharmaceutical industry maintained a high-level growth. The pharmaceutical industry is typically viewed as an industry against the economic circle, i.e. the more sluggish the economic growth is, the greater the demand for medicines will become and the faster the pharmaceutical industry will grow. From January to May 2016, the Industrial value added of the pharmaceutical industry grew 10.2% year on year, 1.0 percentage point higher than the first quarter of this year and 0.3 percentage points higher than the previous year (Fig. 1.16).

Table 1.8 Accumulative growth rates of the food industry's main indicators (*Unit %*)

	Farm and sideline food processing industry				Food manufacturing industry			
	Revenue	Profit	Value of export delivery	Industrial value added	Revenue	Profit	Value of export delivery	Industrial value added
Feb 2015	5.2	8.3	−3.5	5.4	8.3	11.6	2.4	7.1
Mar 2015	3.9	7.9	−3.0	4.8	7.9	11.6	−1.5	6.4
Apr 2015	3.4	9.7	−5.6	4.2	7.3	12.6	−1.4	6.3
May 2015	3.1	11.5	−4.8	4.4	7.1	12.1	−2.2	6.5
Jun 2015	3.7	11.2	−4.3	4.9	7.0	12.8	−3.4	6.8
July 2015	4.0	10.9	−4.3	5.3	6.6	12.0	−1.1	6.8
Aug 2015	4.3	11.7	−3.2	5.5	6.5	11.9	0.5	6.8
Sep 2015	4.3	12.7	−2.5	5.6	6.5	11.8	0.5	7.1
Oct 2015	4.2	12.2	−2.1	5.6	6.5	11.7	0.3	7.2
Nov 2015	4.0	10.1	−3.0	5.6	6.2	9.9	1.4	7.4
Dec 2015	3.5	6.4	−1.8	5.5	6.3	9.1	1.1	7.5
Feb 2016	5.1	14.9	4.2	6.1	8.2	14.8	12.4	9.2
Mar 2016	5.1	12.1	3.1	5.6	7.5	17.5	10.4	8.6
Apr 2016	4.6	12.2	4.2	6.1	7.3	17.6	10.6	8.8
May 2016	5.7	11.7	5.0	6.2	7.8	15.1	10.5	8.7
	Wine, beverage and refined tea manufacturing industry				Tobacco industry			
	Revenue	Profit	Value of export delivery	Industrial value added	Revenue	Profit	Value of export delivery	Industrial value added
Feb 2015	7.8	6.2	−4.1	9.4	5.4	−0.2	−61.6	0.5
Mar 2015	7.0	6.1	0.3	9.5	4.7	−1.1	−21.1	1.1
Apr 2015	6.1	13.9	−0.5	9.3	4.7	1.3	2.3	1.5
May 2015	6.2	13.7	1.5	8.7	5.6	0.0	−7.7	2.5

(continued)

Table 1.8 (continued)

	Wine, beverage and refined tea manufacturing industry				Tobacco industry			
	Revenue	Profit	Value of export delivery	Industrial value added	Revenue	Profit	Value of export delivery	Industrial value added
Jun 2015	6.4	12.3	−5.3	8.2	5.5	−0.4	2.9	3.0
July 2015	6.0	12.4	−5.9	8.0	4.4	−1.4	13.8	2.2
Aug 2015	6.2	10.9	−5.6	7.9	2.0	−0.9	18.1	1.3
Sep 2015	6.7	10.6	−8.8	8.0	3.2	−1.5	10.0	0.9
Oct 2015	7.0	9.9	−9.5	7.8	3.2	−2.1	4.4	1.6
Nov 2015	7.0	9.0	0.1	7.7	3.6	−1.0	2.0	2.3
Dec 2015	6.4	7.5	−1.9	7.7	5.5	−1.4	10.3	3.4
Feb 2016	7.5	11.8	21.5	7.4	−13.1	−17.0	21.4	−15.6
Mar 2016	6.7	12.0	13.4	7.2	−11.1	−17.0	43.3	−13.4
Apr 2016	5.5	5.0	9.4	6.3	−9.5	−18.1	29.1	−12.9
May 2016	5.6	3.0	7.8	6.1	−11.7	−24.0	9.0	−12.0

Source National Bureau of Statistics website

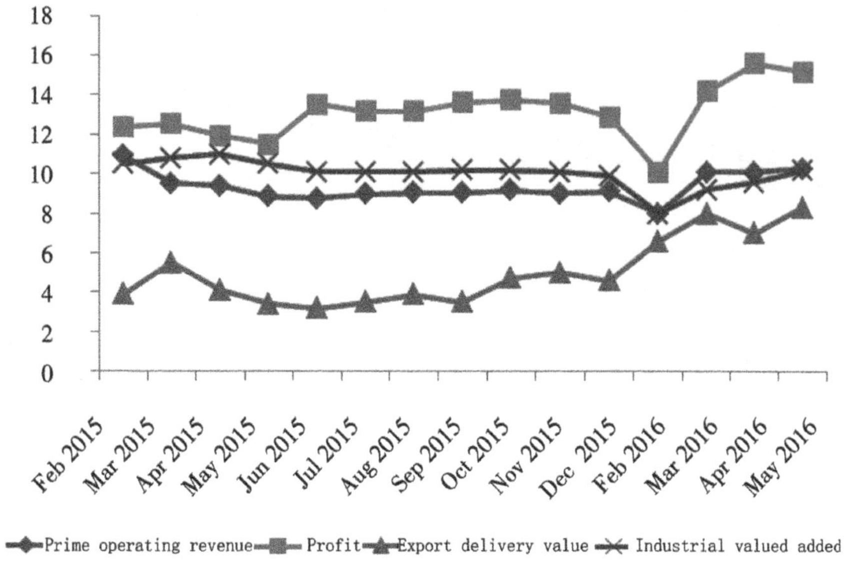

Fig. 1.16 Accumulative growth rate of the pharmaceutical industry's main indicators. *Source* National Bureau of Statistics website

As compared to most industries, the pharmaceutical industry assumes a more positive performance indicator. From January to May 2016, the prime operating revenue and profit of the pharmaceutical industry grew 10.3 and 15.2% year on year respectively, 0.2 and 1.0 percentage point respectively higher than the first quarter of this year, and 1.2 and 2.3 percentage points respectively higher than the previous year. From January to May, the export delivery value of the pharmaceutical industry grew 8.3% year on year, 0.3 percentage point higher than the first quarter of this year and 3.7 percentage points higher than the previous year.

Chapter 2
Forecast and Prospect of Industrial Economics Operation in the Second Half of the Year 2016

Xiouli Wang and Fangfang Li

Variations in the industrial economics operation may take place in tendency and cycle. Since the year of 2010, the growth rate of China's industrial economics seemingly has the tendency towards slowing down. While the tendency variable factors played a leading role in the slowdown of industrial economics operation, the cyclical factors played a key role. Main factors acting on tendency variation included: (i) capital accumulation, (ii) variation in labor force and its qualities, and (iii) technical progress. Cyclical variation was largely subject to short-time simulative monetary and fiscal policy and to variability of requirement space. Currently, due to declining marginal rate of capital return, there would be a downturn in the pace of capital accumulation. Variation in labor force and its qualities took little effect in a short term, but technical progress would hopefully become a supporting factor for this round of industrial economic growths. The drop-offs in global demand and domestic investment constituted a realistic basis for the government to implement a proactive fiscal and monetary policy.

In this report, the time sequence model is used to simulate the growth rates of industrial economics under various circumstances. According to the simulation results, (1) the slowing down tendency will continue; (2) the proactive financial and monetary policy plays a significant role in easing the fluctuations of industrial economics growth; and (3) the technical progress will be the main supporting force for industrial economic growth.

X. Wang (✉) · F. Li
Industrial Economic Situation Analysis Team, Institute of Industrial Economics, CASS, #5 Jianguomennei Street, 100733 Beijing, P.R. China

I.E.S.A.T. Institute of Industrial Economics, CASS (ed.), *Summer Report of China Industrial Economic Situation Analysis (2016)*, Current Chinese Economic Report Series, DOI 10.1007/978-981-10-4690-2_2

2.1 Analysis of the Industrial Economics Prosperity in 2016

To get an intuitive understanding of the industrial economics development, this report has synthesized the available original data including industrial economics development to derive a composite indicator that reflects the situation of industrial economics, i.e. the composite index. According to the composite index, the industrial economics grew significantly in the first quarter of 2016, unlike the trend that remained lower last year. According to the prosperity index, the first quarter of 2016 witnessed a significant rise in prosperity index of industrial economics as compared to the previous year, but the lagging index indicates that this high trend seems feeble and the leading index indicates that this trend will continue.

(1) Formation of the composite index

Processing of original data: the composite index needs to eliminate the "redundant" information (or information irrelative to our purpose) from the original data. To eliminate this "redundant" information, it can be differentiated from original data. Firstly, the original data include high-frequency and low-frequency data, and the former contains daily, weekly and monthly data. What is needed in this report is the monthly data, so daily and weekly data are "redundant" to us and all data are necessarily subject to de-frequency processing. Secondly, the original data contain output data and value quantity data, and the value quantity data may lead to incomparability inside data sequence under the influence of changing prices; therefore, the incomparable data caused by changing prices need to be removed in order to accurately describe the trend of industrial economics development. Thirdly, it is the influence of movable holiday effect. Unlike the statistical data that are calculated in accordance with the solar calendar, the traditional Chinese Spring is always celebrated in accordance with the lunar calendar, so the Spring Festival usually takes place in different solar months. As a public holiday in China, the Spring Festival has strong holiday effects: suspended production, additional leisure time, sharp rise in consumption, and abnormality in all economic activities. As a result, some "redundant" information such as "holiday effect" is included in monthly data. When the data are relevant to growth rate, the above three kinds of information are redundant information that needs to be removed in this report. Thanks to coincidence between seasonal information and holiday information, however, the movable holiday information is usually eliminated earlier than is the seasonable information. In this report, the three kinds of redundant information will be eliminated by de-frequency adjustment, price adjustment and movable holiday adjustment methods.

Index selection: index is selected to acquire original data that can reflect the most of industrial economics trend. The three types of index are required to have an concordance index that reflect the condition of industrial economics development, a leading index that predicts the concordance index, and a lagging index which this report is most concerned with. So far, there are a number of methods for index selection, such as the peak valley alignment method, the cross correlation coefficient method, the K-L information quantity method and the regression analysis method. In this report, the cross correlation coefficient method is used for index selection.

Correlation analysis is a statistical method commonly used in research on closeness among various variables and in research on the degree of correlation between two or more variables and the mutual relation of phenomena with certain functions. The correlative relation means the stochastic relation of change in two phenomena values that are not completely determined, or a kind of dependence relation that is not yet completely determined, often abbreviated as correlative relation, which is the object of study in correlation analysis. The closeness of correlative relation describes the degree of association among variables through calculation of correlation coefficient, i.e. the correlation coefficient is the statistical magnitude that describes the degree and direction of linear relation between two variables, usually expressed as r, without unit, value of which ranges between −1 and +1. The closer to r the absolute value is, the greater the degree of linear correlation between two variables will be. If r is greater than 0, it is a positive correlation and variable Y will increase as variable X increases; if r is less than 0, it is a negative correlation and variable Y will decrease as variable x increases.

Based on the principle of correlation coefficient, the cross correlation coefficient method has broken the sequence of two variables' correlation coefficient arranged by time limit according to time variable. This sequence may give the mutual relation between two variables at different times; accordingly, the maximum cross correlation coefficient is used to determine whether this index is a leading index, concordance index or a lagging index.

Synthesis of index: the composite index may be coded in different ways, e.g. the composite index method of the US Department of Commerce, the composite index method introduced by the Economic Planning Agency of Japan, and the composite index method of the UN Organization for Economic Cooperation and Development (OECD). The Japanese Economic Planning Agency's composite index method agrees with the US Department of Commerce in basic idea but differs slightly in method while the OECD's composite index method is developed specific to the leading composite index and seems simpler than the former two methods. In this report, the US Department of Commerce's composite index method is adopted as an internationally common method. It is basically used in the literature of Chinese development of prosperity index.

Step 1: Determine and standardize the symmetrical change rate of index

(i) Let index Y_{ijt} be the value of j index in i index group at t time, where $i = 1, 2, 3$, representing the leading, concordance and lagging index groups respectively, $j = 1, 2, 3, \ldots, k_i$, representing indexes in three groups, and k_i means the number of indexes in i index group. First determine symmetrical change C_{ijt} of Y_{ijt}, where $t = 2, 3, \ldots, n$.

(ii) To prevent greatly variable indexes from producing significant impact on composite index, the symmetrical change rate C_{ijt} of each index is standardized to make its average absolute value equal to 1. First determine the normalized factor A_{ij} and then standardize C_{ijt} with A_{ij} to obtain standardized change rate S_{ijt}, where $t = 2, 3, \ldots, n$.

Step 2: Determine standardized average change rate of each index group

(i) Determine average change rates of the leading index, concordance index and lagging index group, with $R_{i,t}$ of $i = 1, 2, 3$ and $t = 2, 3, \ldots, n$.
Where W_{ij} is the weight of j index in i index group. The equal weight is usually used to set weight in composite index. The scoring system may be used to determine weight so that each index is given a score according to its economic importance, statistical adequacy, historical concordance and publishing timeliness, and then each index is weighted. If this step is not followed, the weight will be not as desirable as equal weight due to its strong arbitrariness and subjectivity. In order to keep consistent the numerical values of composite index in three index group, the standardized average change rates of all three index groups need to be calculated by dividing the average change rates of all index groups by normalized factor among index groups.
(ii) Work out the normalized factor F_i, where $i = 1, 2, 3$.
(iii) Figure out the standardized average change rate $V_{i,t}$, where $t = 2, 3, \ldots, n$.

Step 3: Calculate composite index

(i) Let $I_i(1) = 100$, then $i = 1, 2, 3$ and $t = 2, 3, \ldots, n$.
(ii) Synthesize a composite index with 100 as benchmark year, where I_i is the average value of $I_{i,t}$ in the benchmark year.

Follow above step in aggregating and synthesizing indexes of three index groups, and then figure out the composite index of the leading index, concordance index and lagging index.

(2) Analysis of prosperity index in the first half of 2016

It is indicated by the leading index and concordance index that the first half of 2016 greeted a slow pickup trend of prosperity from a low level. In January and February 2016, the prosperity of leading index fell into the range of negative values under the influence of sluggish prosperity in 2015 but assumed a constant pickup trend, and it further recovered above zero in March 2016. The concordance index presented a trend ascending year over year and descending month over month. In Fig. 2.1, the prosperity of concordance index ascended for a time to about 0.4 of that in January and descended afterwards to almost zero, but it picked up in March 2016, generally higher than the prosperity in the same period last year, regardless of a descending

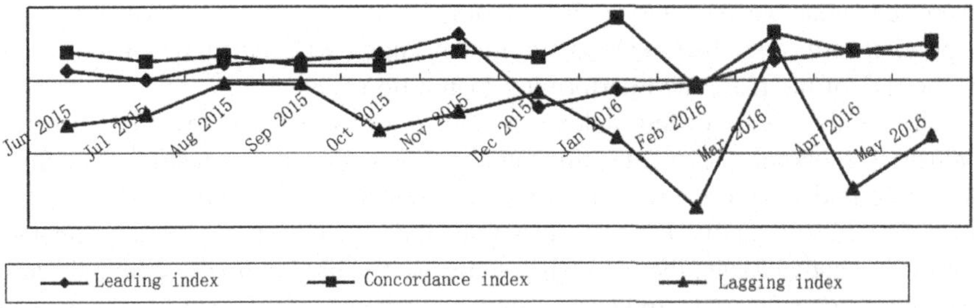

Fig. 2.1 Composite Index of IIE Prosperity Indexes

trend that took place later. The lagging index (mainly including export information and price information) indicated some risks in such growth. In 2016, exclusive of March and June, the prosperity of lagging index remained below zero with a greater degree of fluctuation. For some time in the future, there will be increasing uncertainties about growth of industrial economics.

According to prosperity indicators, (1) the fringe market improved greatly; the PMI of American manufacturing industry bounced back over the threshold; the PMI of Eurozone manufacturing industry maintained above the threshold and assumed an uptrend. The economic situation of developed countries would eventually have effect on China's export trade; despite a substantial decline in China's general trade export volume in the first quarter of 2016, the export volume grew 20% year on year in March; but there had been no substantial growth in the export volume of general trade as the domestic market of China remained in adjustment; (2) the real estate market witnessed brisk trades. In the first half of 2016, the area sold of real estate grew rapidly. From January to June 2016, it reached 643.02 million square meters, growing 27.9% year on year; the sales of real estate amounted to RMB 4.8682 trillion, growing 42.1%. The investment scale of real estate development maintained a moderate-rapid rate of growth; from January to June 2016, it grew 6.1% year on year, indicating a limited role of real estate market in driving industrial growth; (3) there was a slowdown in growth of fixed asset investment and a notable decline in industrial fixed asset investment. From January to June 2016, the fixed asset investment in China amounted to RMB 25.836 trillion (excluding peasant households), with nominal year-on-year growth of 9% (it was actually 11% after adjusting for inflation). The investment in the secondary industry amounted to RMB 10.1702 trillion, growing 4.4%, 16.7 and 7.7 percentage points lower than the primary industry the tertiary industry respectively, where the industrial investment amounted to RMB 9.9594 trillion, growing 4.2% year on year, and the manufacturing investment amounted to RMB 8.2261 trillion, growing 3.3% only; (4) under the influence of overcapacity and inventory adjustment, the outputs of industrial products saw an uneven year-on-year growth, e.g. the outputs of cast iron, crude steel and coke kept sagging while those of ethylene and aluminum products kept growing; and (5) the money supply M1 grew rapidly while M2 slowed down. In response to the downturn risks of industrial economics, Chinese government exercised proactive monetary policy, resulting in a significant growth in money supply; nevertheless, the growth rate of money supply M2 tended to slow down due to the risk of the rising non-performing loan ratio (Table 2.1).

The steady rise in leading indexes predicted a quarter-long slow growth of the industrial economics for some time in the future, but the industrial economics would be under big downward pressure as it remained in growing pains of rebalance. Specifically, firstly, the ex-factory price index of industrial products remained within a negative range, the industrial overcapacity failed to improve in real sense, and the main industrial products trading market was not as active as expected; secondly, this round of growth of industrial economics was still dependent heavily on pickup of real estate market, and there would be limited space for growth in the future as the real estate market entered the period of adjustment; thirdly, the fixed asset investment remained a main force in supporting this round of slow growth of industrial economics, and the main sectors that could drive growth of fixed asset investment were infrastructure investment and real estate market investment while the manufacturing fixed asset investment remained at a low level; and fourthly, the loose monetary policy played a positive role in promoting pickup of real estate market, but the exit of the loose monetary policy would inevitably restrain the growing trend of the real estate market and further compromise demands of industrial products. Generally, this round of industrial economics growth as a continuity of the old investment-driven development pattern failed to result in any new growth points. Considering the transition of China's economic development from the industry-driven pattern to the service-driven pattern, there would be an irresistible trend of rapid growth of the service industry and slowdown of industrial growth.

2.2 Factors Influencing the Trend Variation of Industrial Economics

The decline of fixed asset investment in industrial sectors would inevitably lead to a slowing growth rate of capital stock and usher in a falling trend of industrial sectors. The innovative development strategy and global technological revolution initiated by Chinese Government would be a strong support for growth of industrial economics.

(1) Lower and lower investment return of industrial enterprises and continuous downsizing of the fixed asset investment

Since reform and opening up in 1979, the profit scale of Chinese industrial sectors had expanded constantly; especially since the year of 2002, it grew at a rate up to 20% and made it possible for industrial investment return to maintain a high level. Since the year of 2011, however, the profit growth rate of industrial sectors slowed down even to a negative rate. As the profit growth rate remained low, the

Table 2.1 Year-on-year variations of prosperity indexes (*unit* %)

Name of index		Dec 2015	Jan 2016	Feb 2016	Mar 2016	Apr 2016	May 2016
Leading indexes	Output of coke	−14.13	−2.56	−17.64	−5.11	−3.15	−0.32
	Output of aluminum products	14.37	10.51	22.86	15.20	12.05	11.07
	Output of ethylene	−5.50	4.81	16.53	10.96	19.51	16.51
	Output of cast iron	−6.88	−15.44	−5.99	−0.08	−1.80	−0.51
	Output of crude steel	−3.88	−11.66	−1.79	−1.63	0.74	0.79
	Number of new projects commenced in the current year that utilized fixed asset investment	15.65	47.50	63.98	30.80	30.01	24.48
	Total planned investment in construction projects in the current year that utilized fixed asset investment	−6.07	6.57	17.90	−17.84	18.28	−3.11
	Area sold of commodity houses	1.64	22.09	35.73	37.66	44.05	24.25
	Area of commodity houses under construction	−22.88	0.83	12.09	3.66	4.65	−1.42
	Composite index of Shanghai Stock Exchange	9.41	−14.73	−18.80	−19.85	−33.85	−36.76
	Composite index of Shenzhen Stock Exchange	14.98	−15.54	−22.63	−20.56	−31.56	−36.90
	Money supply M2	11.56	11.96	10.75	10.85	10.30	9.61%
	American manufacturing PMI[a]	48	48.2	49.5	51.8	50.8	51.3
	Eurozone manufacturing PMI[a]	53.2	52.3	51.2	51.6	51.7	51.5
Concordance indexes	Industrial value added	5.90	0.38	11.60	6.80	6.00	6.00
	Electricity production	0.16	25.35	−16.00	5.94	−0.13	1.62
	Import volume of general trade	−8.99	−23.27	−14.94	−9.23	−10.68	2.19
	Total investment in real estate development	−3.42	−3.62	6.63	7.21	7.24	4047
	M1–MO	15.50	17.22	20.75	23.20	23.81	24.78

(continued)

Table 2.1 (continued)

Name of index		Dec 2015	Jan 2016	Feb 2016	Mar 2016	Apr 2016	May 2016
Lagging indexes	Export volume of general trade	−0.25	−9.28	−30.19	20.06	−0.52	−4.47
	Ex-factory price indexes of industrial products (EFPI)	94.1	94.7	95.1	95.7	96.6	97.2
	Consumer price index (CPI)[a]	101.6	101.8	102.3	102.3	102.3	102

Notes
1. Indexes asterisked with "a" are original values while other indexes are year-on-year growth rates after price adjustment in that month
2. Indexes without January and February data are interpolated by growth rate calculation and workday calculation

investment return receded gradually. Bai Chong'en and Zhang Qiong (2014)[1] pointed out that since the year 2011 China's return on invested capital presented a constantly declining trend, i.e. 21.1, 16.6 and 14.7% respectively from 2011 to 2013. The return on invested capital of industrial sectors stayed basically consistent with that of the whole society. The former's decline would result in transfer of investment into other industries and into overseas market. Data showed that from 2005 to 2013, the fixed asset investment of industrial sectors took up all the time over 40% of the total fixed assets investment; however, since the year of 2014, the fixed asset fell back to 39.9% and presented a trend of continuous decline (Fig. 2.2).

The growth of private fixed asset investment ushered in this round of the declining trend in fixed asset investment. Over years, the growth of private fixed asset investment in the secondary industry has all the time outnumbered the growth of total fixed asset investment and thus become the main force of fixed asset investment in the secondary industry. In March 2016, however, the private fixed asset investment in the secondary industry began to present a declining trend and became a leading force to bring down the growth of fixed asset investment (Fig. 2.3).

The declining fixed asset investment in industrial sectors would inevitably lead to a slowing growth rate of capital stock and usher in a falling trend of industrial sectors. According to the new-classic growth theory, a country's output depends on its capital stock, labor and total factor productivity; capital equals last year's capital stock minus depreciation and plus investment; when the investment size is greater than depreciation, the capital stock increases annually; when the investment size is equal to depreciation, the capital stock sees a zero growth rate; when the investment

[1]Bai Chong'en and Zhang Qiong: Analysis of China's Investment Return and Influencing Factors, World Economy, Issue 10, 2014.

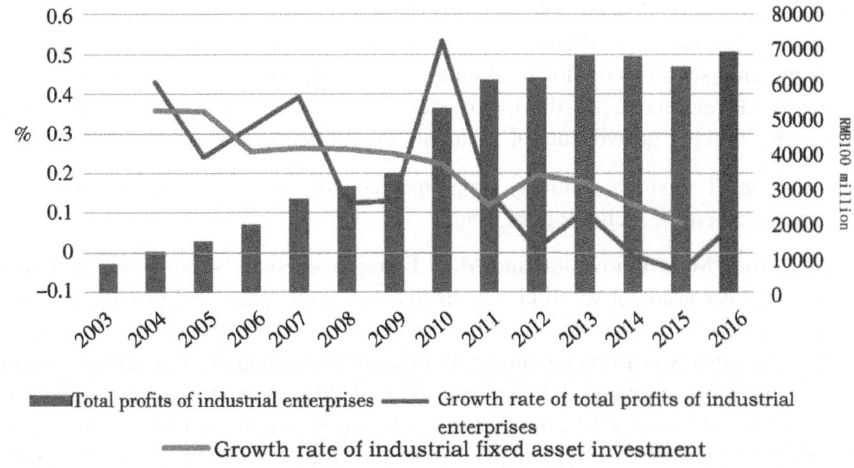

Fig. 2.2 Profits and fixed asset investment of industrial enterprises from 2003 to 2016. *Notes 1* Data are sourced from National Bureau of Statistics. *2* Total profits of 2016 are predicted values. *3* The primary coordinate axis gives values of growth rate while the secondary coordinate axis provides values of investment size

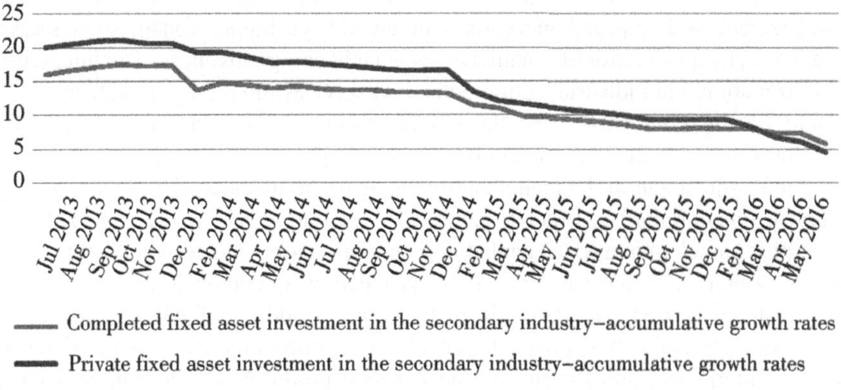

Fig. 2.3 Tendency chart for fixed asset investment in the secondary industry since July 2013 (*unit %*). *Source* National Bureau of Statistics website

size is smaller than depreciation, the capital stock suffers a negative growth rate; the greater the size of capital stock, the greater the size of depreciation; and a zero growth rate results inevitably when there is an unchanged investment size. Currently, however, the capital stock declines annually as the investment size shrinks annually; the capital stock moves rapidly towards a zero growth rate, even a negative one. If other production factors remain unchanged, there will be a positive correlation between capital stock and output, and a slowing or even a negative growth rate of capital stock will lead directly to a slowing or a negative growth rate of output. The slowing growth of capital stock is an inexorable law of economic development, so the slowdown of output also suggests an inevitable trend of economic development. As the fixed asset investment in industrial sectors slows down, the slowing growth rate of industrial output becomes more apparent.

(2) National innovative strategy implemented to provide strong support for improvement of technological level

In 2015, the "Mass Innovation and Mass Entrepreneurship" strategy was initiated by Chinese government to eliminate institutional constraints and provide support for startup of new enterprises, development of new products and expansion of new markets by all types of market entities through implementation of structural reform and institutional innovation. In the first half of 2015, Chinese government also issued *Made in China 2025*, the first ten-year action guiding document for manufacturing industry that specified nine strategic tasks for Chinese manufacturing industry, such as improving the innovation capacity, promoting in-depth integration of information and industrialization, enhancing quality brand and achieving breakthroughs in key fields. The development strategy to improve the innovation capacity of manufacturing industry underlined technology innovation and business model innovation in enterprises, with the former usually focused on breakthrough in a certain process while the latter combined advanced technology with advanced management and required enterprises to be always highly sensitive to market condition changes in order to maintain sustainable competitiveness. The integration of information and industrialization embodied services offered by manufacturers; it would be the only choice for the manufacturing industry to begin integrative development with the service industry in a certain stage; during upgrading and structural adjustment of the manufacturing industry, more enterprises opted to adopt "service outsourcing" in order to consolidate resources and make use of unique strengths; namely, enterprises tended to maintain sectors with core competitiveness and outsource such service activities as production, operation and even management usually carried out internally in the upper, middle and lower processes of production activities, thus providing development opportunities for some producer service enterprises; and the integration between producer service enterprises and industrial manufacturers helped improve the resources utilization efficiency and the industrial efficiency. A famous brand is the product of independent innovation capacity. Since the "11th Five-Year Plan" (2006–2010), the famous brand development strategy has created a large number of famous brands with strong competitiveness; as a globally influential big power in the world, however, China is currently short of self-owned famous brands with international competitiveness; therefore, building quality brand is an effective measure for China to further its independent innovation capacity and protect intellectual property. The core of the "Mass Innovation and Mass Entrepreneurship" strategy and *Made in China 2025* initiative still lies in innovation that has played a positive role in vitalizing market and starting up businesses. In the second half of 2016, all economic sectors will issue and implement several policy measures supporting this core and specialized planning for subdivided fields to provide strong support for improvement of technological level.

(3) Global disruptive technologies developed to become an external force to propel industrial innovation

The advanced manufacturing technologies such as robot and 3D printing, the information technologies such as cloud computation, Internet of Things and big data, the new resource technologies such as renewable energy sources and advanced oil-gas exploration, the biotechnologies such as a new generation of genome, and the intelligent technologies such as auto-driving vehicles and knowledge-based office automation have exerted far-reaching influence on the world industry; in particular, these technologies have generated profound changes in the production mode, the development pattern, the industrial type and organizational form of the manufacturing industry, and pushed development of the manufacturing industry towards intelligent, service, collaborative, network and green manufacturing. Specifically, the new generation of information technology has permeated into all aspects of the manufacturing value chain, including changes in technology and manufacturing mode, and thus promoted reconstruction of the manufacturing value chain; the application of the Internet of Things has enabled manufacturers to achieve real-time acquisition of information and real-time monitoring of production process; the application of big data has enabled manufacturers to identify and solve invisible problems and predict the future development; the application of cloud computation has helped manufacturers predict market demands and consumers' individual needs and achieved precise location of target consumer group, so it has been constantly putting right the strategic direction and altering the organizational and operational patterns of manufacturers; the combination of the Internet of Things and 3D printing has promoted establishment of new manufacturers that will clone things by reading information; the development of robot technology has made production lines become more automatic, standard and refined, and may further create "unmanned factory", thus providing infinite opportunities for traditional manufacturing industry; and the steady development of advanced manufacturing technologies has resulted in effective integration of manufacturing information and intelligence. In this process, the renewable energy source technology has provided a solid foundation for green development of the manufacturing industry while the 3D printing technology that has saved more materials, improved the utilization rate of raw materials and made materials used more environment friendly when manufacturing products may push the manufacturing industry towards sustainable and healthy development. Currently, breakthroughs have been achieved in some disruptive technologies in China. In the future, with wide applications of these technologies, their economic potentialities will be released and become main driving force to improve industrial technological level.

2.3 Factors Influencing Cyclical Variation of Industrial Economics

The cyclical fluctuation of industrial economics in the future will be subject to factors such as global economic recovery and changes in both national and international demands, and will therefore lead to cyclical variations of industrial economics. Various uncertainties will likely result in drastic fluctuation in the future industrial economics.

(1) Sluggish global economy recovery and significant global trade slow down

Since the year of 2008, the growth of global international trade slowed down under the influence of financial crisis. Despite various incentive policies that simulated economic growth in 2010 and 2011, the zero or even negative growth trend remained unchanged (see Fig. 2.4).

Economic differentiation continued in main economies of the world. The American economy saw a steady recovery and assumed a trend of slight growth. The European economy was recovering from European debt crisis and moving towards stabilization. The emerging economies witnessed obvious internal differentiation; India maintained a steady economic growth while Russia and Brazil suffered a negative growth. On the whole, the international economic situation has slightly improved, but the global economic growth still featured a too slow, fragile and unbalanced recovery. The US dollars appreciation and continuous decline of international oil price added more uncertainties to global financial markets and global economic recovery, such as intensification of global trade protection,

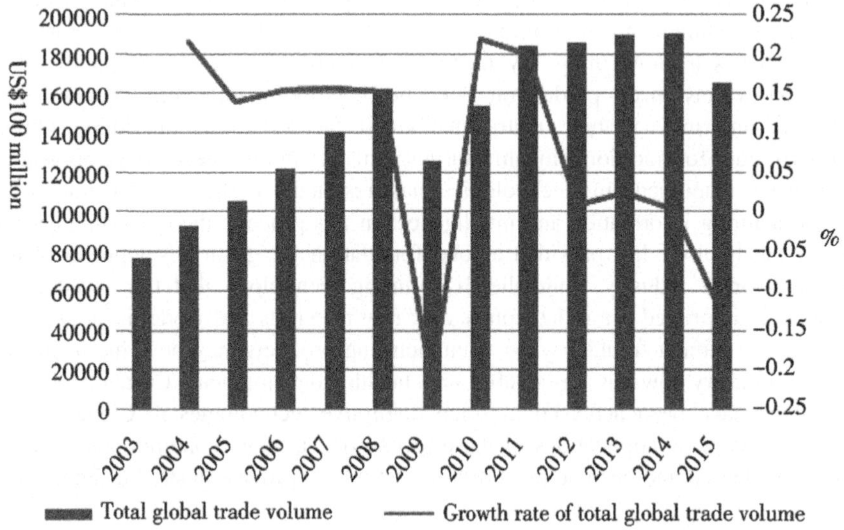

Fig. 2.4 Global trade scale since the year of 2003

expansion of exchange rate fluctuations, local economic upheaval and geopolitical tensions. Continuous changes of the world economic pattern have brought about huge risks and impact on China's foreign trade and restriction on China's external demands. In addition, the "Road and Belt" strategy involves many sensitive regions in Western Asia and Eastern Europe, so the geopolitical tensions may have adverse effects on China's overseas investment under the background of the Belt and Road Initiative and to some extent compromise industrial growth that should be stimulated by the Belt and Road Initiative.

(2) Challenges facing China's industrial goods trade though its competitiveness improves constantly

In the international trade pattern, China's industrial goods took up an increasingly high proportion. In 2003, China's industrial goods only took up 5.7% of global goods trade, but the proportion rose to 13.8% in 2015, steadily increasing in more than ten years. Under the influence of shrinking global trade, China's export growth rate slowed down and trade scale also withered, but China's trade competitiveness witnessed a rising trend year by year; it is predicted that the rising trend of trade proportion will persist in 2016.

The comparative advantages of China's industrial development are under various threats and interruptive risks. The competitive advantages of China's industrial enterprises have over years depended on low-cost advantages based on low-level production factors. With the loss of demographic dividend, the rise of domestic factor cost, the intensification of resource and environment pressure and the expansion of economic scale, however, this low-cost advantage is diminishing little by little and the dividend in trade that uses low cost as the main competitiveness basically comes to an end. In addition, new advantages based on the high-level product factors can hardly be established in a short time and may interrupt competitive advantages, resulting in depression of industrial goods export, slowdown of economic growth rate and decline of enterprises' international competitiveness. In contrast, some emerging economies, such as Southeast Asian and African countries, have lower labor cost than China, and the comparative advantages of labor force in these countries have come into market, tending to supersede China's traditional advantages. In addition, the advanced manufacturing technology, information technology, biotechnology and energy technology spread quickly over the world and are widely used by developed countries to exploit potential markets and realize "backflow of manufacturing industry" and "reindustrialization". The "backflow of manufacturing industry" and "reindustrialization" strategy of developed countries has enabled them to slow down overseas transfer of their manufacturing industries, especially the high-end manufacturing industries. The development of China's hi-tech industries depends largely on the international market, so it will be more difficult for China to borrow technologies from developed countries; instead, China will rely on its financing cost, logistics cost and tax cost as well as the technological gap.

(3) The effect of regional collaborative strategy of "Beijing-Tianjin-Hebei integration", "Yangtze River Economic Belt" and the Belt and Road Initiative to provide huge demand space for industrial development

In March 2015, the *Vision and Actions on Jointly Building the Silk Road Economic Belt and the 21st-Century Maritime Silk Road* was issued jointly by the National Development and Reform Commission (NDRC), Ministry of Foreign Affairs and Ministry of Commerce to promote construction of the Belt and Road Initiative. In April 2015, the *Coordinated Development Program for Beijing-Tianjin-Hebei Region* was adopted at the meeting of the Political Bureau of the CPC Central Committee. In October 2015, *China's 13th Five-Year Plan (2016–2020) on National Economic and Social Development*, adopted at the Fifth Plenary Session of the 18th Communist Party of China (CPC) Central Committee, proposed formation of the lengthwise and crosswise economic axial belt along the coast, the river and the line guided by the Belt and Road Initiative construction, Beijing-Tianjin-Hebei coordinated development and Yangtze River Economic Belt construction and based on the overall strategy of regional development, and formation of city clusters including the northeast region, the central plains region, the middle reaches of the Yangtze River region, the Chengdu-Chongqing region and the central Shaanxi region through prior development of such city clusters as Beijing-Tianjin-Hebei, the Yangtze River Delta and the Pearl River Delta.

The new demand space for China's industrial development provided by the regional coordinated development strategy along with its policy effect has brought indefinite opportunities for China's industrial development in the next year. Firstly, the strategy has driven the balanced development in these regions. For a long time, Chinese government's focus on coastal regions for economic development has create many economic hot spots in the eastern regions with most advanced economic development and most sufficient utilization of funds; in contrast, the central and western regions, especially the western regions, saw a rather low fund utilization rate and a narrow extent of opening up to the outside world due to their location, which laid severe restrictions on economic development but indicated potential industrial demands. The formation of city clusters has led to industrial cluster effect and creation of an industrial development pattern in which the growth poles of Beijing and Shanghai will drive economic growth in surrounding provinces, favorable for optimization of urban spatial layout, coordination among industrial sectors and expansion of environmental capacity and ecological space; in particular, the "Yangtze River Economic Belt" covering 11 provinces and cities has linked together the eastern, central and western regions to form a coordinated development belt that allows interaction and cooperation among the eastern and western regions and drives economic development in the western region, has fundamentally changed the location conditions of the western regions as many provinces along the Belt and Road Initiative are located in West China, has broadened the opening-up extent in China's northwestern and southwestern regions and provided opportunities for these regions to carry out foreign trade and foreign investment activities and achieve leap-forward development. Then, the strategy has driven investment in infrastructure construction. In the regional coordinated development strategy, the infrastructure construction is the foundation and top priority as it provides convenience for inter-regional communication. In the *Coordinated Development Program for Beijing-Tianjin-Hebei Region*, it was proposed that RMB 4.2 trillion investments be put into Beijing-Tianjin-Hebei integration in the future six years, with most of which will be invested in infrastructure construction. Huge demand of infrastructure investment in western countries along the Belt and Road Initiative will inevitably drive China's investment in infrastructure construction. Meanwhile, severe overcapacity problems of Chinese industry in capital construction, such as cutthroat competition among enterprises, have led to waste of enormous resources and a series of social problems. The advancement of the Belt and Road Initiative has found new outlets for China's overcapacities so that Chinese enterprises will have to promote industrial transformation and upgrading, improve industrial competitiveness and adjust industrial structure when they decide to "go out".

(4) Debt risks accumulated to pin down industrial operation

Local debt risk remains high. During economic deceleration, the fiscal revenue growth will slow down and the expenditure will rise moderately under the influence of economic fundamentals, enlarging the scale of deficit and debt. Furthermore, the fact that local governments may execute debt financing on various financing platforms to maintain goals of local economic and social development and to accelerate infrastructure construction will initiate a new mode to stimulate economic growth by governments' leveraging investment. When the government no long provides any guarantee for these debts, some of the debts will be transferred by financing platforms to debts payable by the government; as a result, the debts payable by the local government will increase. According to the results of national debt audit at the end of 2015, RMB 1.9 trillion debts payable by the government fell due in 2015. Excessive debt ratio of the local government will put local government under heavy pressure to discharge debts and will also easily lead to crisis of local government debts; in addition, due to different rates of local economic growth and different debt burden of provinces, it is likely to incur local debt crisis. Excessive local government debts may also lead to risk of local government's bankruptcy and place strict restrictions on local government's further financing and on continuous investment in infrastructure construction and thus compromise the growth of industrial economics.

Potential risk in industrial sectors remains high. In May 2016, the debt-to-asset ratio of industrial enterprises above designated size was 56.8%, 0.6 percentage point higher than December 2015, and the leverage ratio reached up to 131%, which increased the operating risk of industrial sectors. It is noted that the excessively high leverage ratio of Chinese enterprises was questioned as the leverage ratio of foreign enterprises maintained at around 70%. In effect, the leverage ratio of Chinese enterprises has been extremely high for many years, for it was closely related to Chinese economic reality: (i) high saving rate that means relatively adequate supply of capitals in China, and (ii) high leverage that results from two realistic bases—relatively lagging development of China's capital market and credit financing used as the main financing channel by China's industrial sectors. However, these two bases are slowly collapsing as the consumer savings declines and the capital market expands and plays more financing functions. In recent years, the de-leverage ratio of industrial enterprises has paced up, reducing from 178% at the beginning of 1998 to 128% at the end of December 2015. The current uptrend of leverage has no realistic base. Furthermore, the local government's debt risks are constantly discharged. China as a whole suffers a very high debt ratio, so the increasing leverage will intensify the risk pressure.

2.4 Prediction of Industrial Growth Trend

HP filtering method adopted in this report separates the growth trend of industrial value added year on year from cyclical factors to analyze roles of different factors in industrial value added. According to the results, the growth rate of industrial economics has slowed down since the year of 2010; the slowing growth rate has continued in the first half of 2016 but the decreasing amplitude was narrowing; and it is predicted that the industrial growth will highly likely hit the bottom in the second half of 2016.

(1) Data source and interpolation of missing values

In this report, the value added year-on-year growth data of industries above designated size are used as observing indicators of industrial growth, with the samples ranging between January 2008 and June 2016. Data are sourced from National Bureau of Statistics website. The industrial value added year-on-year growth rate is: (i) calculated by comparable prices, independent of price factors and free from price adjustment, and (ii) value added growth data of industries above designated size with January growth data missed, which needs interpolation. The traceability method is adopted in this report to interpolate data. Specific steps are as follows.

Firstly, the monthly year-on-year growth rate data and the monthly accumulative growth rate data of industrial value added as well as the monthly actual data in 2005 of industrial value added[2] are obtained from National Bureau of Statistics website. Secondly, the monthly industrial value actually added in 2005 is used to figure out the monthly accumulative growth rates of industrial value added in 2005. Thirdly, the monthly accumulative industrial value added in 2005 and the monthly accumulative growth rates of industrial value added in 2006 are used to calculate the monthly accumulative industrial value added in 2006, and by analogy get the monthly accumulative industrial value added from 2007 to 2016 with January data missed. Fourthly, the monthly industrial value actually added in 2005 and the

[2]Data source: China Monthly Economic Indicators, January 2016.

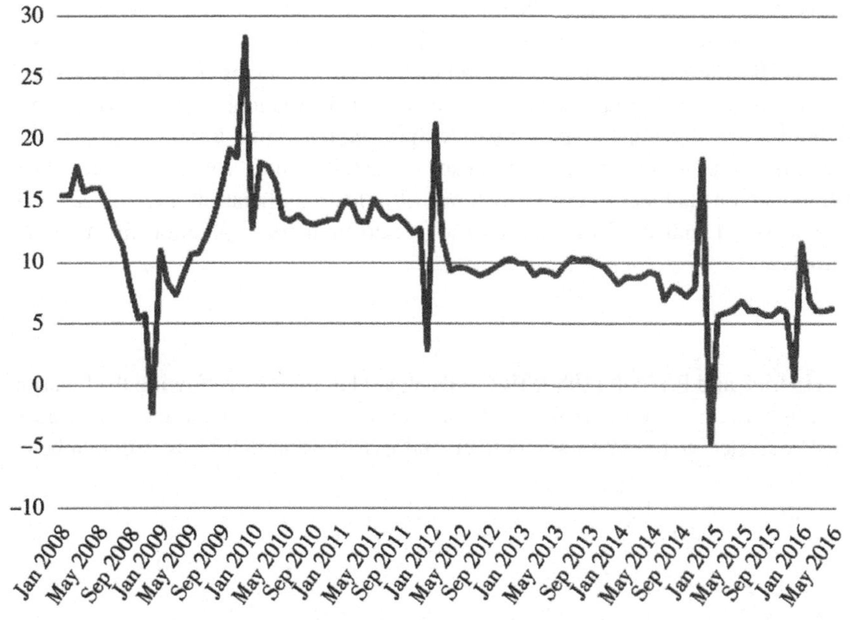

Fig. 2.5 Industrial value added year-on-year growth rates of industries above designated size (%). *Data source* Reckoned from National Bureau of Statistics Website and *China Monthly Economic Indicators*

monthly year-on-year growth rates of industrial value added in 2006 are used to figure out the monthly industrial value actually added in 2006, and by analogy get the monthly industrial value actually added from 2007 to 2016 with January data missed. Fifthly, the industrial values actually added in January from 2006 to 2013 are obtained by the accumulative number in February of industrial value added from 2006 to 2016 with January data missed minus the actual industrial value added in February from 2006 to 2016. Finally, all monthly data calculated above are used to directly get the missing January data about the monthly year-on-year growth rates of industrial value added (Fig. 2.5).

(2) Trend components and fluctuating components of industrial growth separated by HP filtering method

In order to separate the long-term trend factors from the cyclical (irregular) factors of industrial growth and obtain estimation of unobservable potential factors, either the moving average method or the frequency domain estimation method may be used for the original data of single time sequence; the filtering method has a unique advantage, i.e. simple, intuitive and easy for implementation, and can also avoid the problem caused by production function method, i.e. whether the product function can be stable in the economic transition period, and the problem caused by variable structure decomposition method, i.e. whether there exists the Phillips curve of conventional form in China. Therefore, the HP filtering method is adopted in this section to predict the growth trend of industrial economics.

The HP filtering de-trending method may regard economic operation as a certain combination of potential growth and short-term fluctuations and use metrological technology to decompose the actually output sequence into trend components and cyclical components; the former means potential output while the latter means output gap or fluctuation. For growth rate of industrial operation, the time sequence y_t consists of industrial operation trend g_t and industrial operation fluctuation c_t, namely:

$$y_t = g_t + c_t \quad t = 1, \ldots T \tag{2.1}$$

Hodrick and Prescott (1980, 1997)[3] designed HP filter by following the logarithm data moving average method. The filter can obtain a smooth sequence g_t from the time sequence y_t, i.e. trend component, and g_t is the solution to the formula below:

$$Min\left\{\sum_{t=1}^{T}(y_t - g_t)^2 + \lambda\sum_{t=1}^{T}[(g_t - g_{t-1})(g_t - g_{t-2})]\right\} \tag{2.2}$$

where, $\sum_{t=1}^{T}(y_t - g_t)^2$ represents fluctuations, $\sum_{t=1}^{T}[(g_t - g_{t-1})(g_t - g_{t-2})]$ represents trend, and λ is smooth parameter with a positive value used to adjust proportions of fluctuation and trend. Selection of the smooth parameter λ is an important problem in the HP filtering method. Different smooth parameters mean different filters that determine different fluctuating modes and smoothness. According to Hodrick and Prescott (1980, 1997), the value of smooth parameter is taken as 100 in processing annual data, as 1600 in processing quarterly data and as 14,400 in processing monthly data. According to Ravn and Uhlig (2002),[4] the smooth parameter should be 4th power of the observed data frequency, i.e. 6.25 for annual data, 1600 for quarterly data and 129,600 for monthly data. In this report, the data used are growth rates of industrial value added from January 2010 to September 2015, sourced from National Bureau of Statistics website. It is important to note that the missing data on growth rates of industrial value added in January on National Bureau of Statistics website are supplemented by point linear interpolation in this report. Above two types of filters are selected for use in this report: $\lambda = 14{,}400$ and $\lambda = 129{,}600$.

After quarterly adjustment of data, two filters with smooth parameters $\lambda = 14{,}400$ and $\lambda = 129{,}600$ (hereinafter referred to as Filter 1 and Filter 2) are used to filter the natural logarithm of China's industrial value added growth rates and then get the trend components and fluctuation components therein, as illustrated in Fig. 2.6.

---

[3]Hodrick, R., and Prescott, Edward C. (1980, 1997), "Postwar U.S. Business Cycles: An Empirical Investigation", Journal of Money, Credit, and Banking, 29 (1): 1–16.

[4]Ravn, M., and Uhlig H. (2002), "On Adjusting the HP Filter for the Frequency of Observations", Review of Economics and Statistics, 84 (3): 71–75.

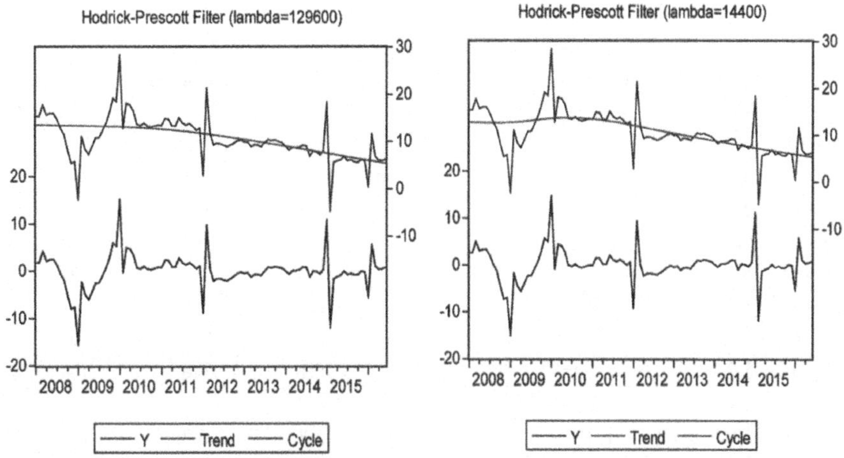

Fig. 2.6 Filtering results of different filters. *Picture source* Eviews 5.0 output result

According to Fig. 2.6, there is no significant difference in trend sequence and fluctuation sequence achieved by two filters, and there is no difference in two trend sequences and two fluctuation sequences as both passed t test of 95% confidence level. Intuitively from the tendency of trend sequences, the potential growth rates of China's industrial operation has been on a curve declining trend all the time since the year of 2008.

(3) Growth forecast and scenario analysis of industrial economics

With the current technological level, China's industrial economics will be highly likely to maintain a slow-down growth rate from the second half of 2016 to the first half of 2017, providing the current monetary and fiscal policies remain unchanged. According to the model prediction, the growth rate of China's industrial economics will reduce to 5.7% at the end of 2016 and to 5.6% in June 2017. Under the influence of moving holidays, obvious fluctuations will occur in industrial growth in January and February 2017; in remaining months of 2017, the industrial economics will operate smoothly.

Benchmark: The quantities and qualities of labor force remain unchanged; the fixed asset investment maintain current development trend; the technical level remains unchanged; and the fiscal and monetary policies remain unchanged.

Scenario 1: The quantities and qualities of labor force remain unchanged; the fixed asset investment maintain current development trend; the technical level remains unchanged; and the fiscal and monetary policy strength is 20% lower than the current level.

Scenario 2: The quantities and qualities of labor force remain unchanged; the fixed asset investment maintain current development trend; the technical level remains unchanged; and the fiscal and monetary policy strength increases 20% over the current level.

Table 2.2 Forecast of industrial growth rates under different scenarios

Year-on-year growth rates of industrial value added (%)						
	Trend value	Fluctuating value	Benchmark	Scenario 1	Scenario 2	Scenario 3
Jan-16	5.9	−5.5	0.4	0.4	0.4	0.4
Feb-16	5.8	5.8	11.6	11.6	11.6	11.6
Mar-16	5.7	1.1	6.8	6.8	6.8	6.8
Apr-16	5.6	0.4	6.0	6.0	6.0	6.0
May-16	5.5	0.5	6.0	6.0	6.0	6.0
Jun-16	5.4	0.8	6.2	6.2	6.2	6.2
Jul-16	5.3	1.3	6.6	6.3	6.8	7.6
Aug-16	5.2	1.2	6.4	6.1	6.6	7.4
Sep-16	5.1	1.1	6.2	6.0	6.4	7.2
Oct-16	5.0	1.0	6.0	5.8	6.2	7.0
Nov-16	4.9	1.0	5.9	5.7	6.1	6.9
Dec-16	4.8	1.0	5.7	5.6	5.9	6.7
Jan-17	4.7	0.9	5.6	5.4	5.8	6.6
Feb-17	4.6	0.9	5.5	5.3	5.7	6.4
Mar-17	4.5	0.9	5.4	5.2	5.5	6.2
Apr-17	4.4	0.9	5.2	5.1	5.4	6.1
May-17	4.2	0.9	5.1	4.9	5.3	5.9
Jun-17	4.1	0.9	5.0	4.8	5.1	5.8

Data source Based on Eviews 5.0 output results

Scenario 3: The quantities and qualities of labor force remain unchanged; the fixed asset investment maintain current development trend; the fiscal and monetary policies remain unchanged; and the technical level increases 20% over the current level (Table 2.2).

According to the results, (1) the industrial growth rate will reduce to 5.7% at the end of 2016 and to 5.0% in June 2017, providing the technical level and investment scale remain unchanged and the current fiscal and monetary policies are maintained; (2) the industrial growth rate will reduce to 5.6% at the end of 2016 and to 4.8% in June 2017, providing the technical level and investment scale remain unchanged and the negative fiscal and monetary policies are implemented; (3) the industrial growth rate will reduce to 5.9% at the end of 2016 and to 5.1% in June 2017, providing the technical level and investment scale remain unchanged and the proactive fiscal and monetary policies are implemented; and (4) the industrial growth rate will reduce to 6.7% at the end of 2016 and to 5.8% in June 2017, providing other factors remain unchanged and the technical level has significantly improved.

Chapter 3
Policy Suggestions for China's Industrial Operation

Qunhui Huang and Hangyan Zhang

With implementation of a series of policies including the supple-side structural reform, the national economy operated quite well and stabilized in slow growth and slow recovery in the first half of 2016. However, the recovery seems not so optimistic in the pessimistic context of the international situation that might complicate and intensify China's industrial economy and might lead to heavier downturn pressure on economic operation in the second half of 2016 as a number of contradictions and risks stand out. In this case, we need to seize the new normal opportunity for economic development, steady growth by taking effective measures against various risks and challenges, promote reform and transformation, break institutional barriers and combine long-term policies with short-term ones, macro policies with micro ones and supply management with demand management so as to pave the way for healthy development of China's industrial economics.

3.1 Focus on Steady Growth and Maintain Relative Stability of Macro Policy

Sharp fluctuations in economic growth are usually traceable back to sharp fluctuations in macro policies. As China's industrial economics are currently "stabilizing in slow growth", sharp fluctuations in macro policies should be avoided as taboos. In the first year of the "13th Five-Year Plan" (2016–20), we need to maintain relative stability and continuity of macro policies, minimize frequent short-term macroeconomic control, deepen the concept of "interval control", give play to the decisive roles of resource allocation in market and shift strategic focus to reform

Q. Huang (✉) · H. Zhang
Industrial Economic Situation Analysis Team, Institute of Industrial Economics, CASS, #5 Jianguomennei Street, 100734 Beijing, P.R. China

I.E.S.A.T. Institute of Industrial Economics, CASS (ed.), *Summer Report of China Industrial Economic Situation Analysis (2016)*, Current Chinese Economic Report Series, DOI 10.1007/978-981-10-4690-2_3

and adjustment of economic structure so that macro policies are authentic in promoting steady growth.

Firstly, we need to stabilize and avoid sharp fluctuations in real estate market. Such actions will be of great importance to economic growth and social stability. During the supply-side reform, de-stocking policies might be most intensive in real estate market; in just two dozen days since February 2016, five bombshell measures were issued by more than ten ministries and committees including the Central Bank of China and National Development and Reform Commission (NDRC), almost one real estate policy being issued per week. In such a context, the government should be active to direct and guide the expectations and behaviors of commercial banks and social public by means of various policy tools to prevent against sharp fluctuations in real estate market and insure stable, healthy development of the real estate market.

Then, we need to continue with proactive fiscal policy and steady monetary policy. Under the pressure of continuous economic downturn, we will implement proactive fiscal policy for tax abatement and increase of social security expenditure, provide support for enterprises in technical transformation and innovation investment and give play to the leading role of governmental investment, guide funds to flow into fields that may generate higher investment efficiency, guarantee implementation of state-approved projects, increase expenditure in unemployment insurance and low-income population, maintain social stability, and create a macro environment to the benefit of structural adjustment, exercise steady monetary policy, duly cut down on interest and reserve and bring down enterprises' financing cost pursuant to economic recovery; in addition, relevant authorities should delivery policy signals in time to market so as to stabilize expectation and confidence on the stock market.

Finally, we need to renovate the methods of macroeconomic regulation and control, strengthen interval control and opportunistic control, make the best of policy tools such as industry, investment and price as well as the fiscal and monetary policies, and take measures for structural reform and especially for supply-side structural reform to prevent all risks and create a favorable environment for economic development.

3.2 Continue to Deepen Supply-Side Reform and Stimulate New Vitality of Industrial Growth

The supply-side reform's emphasis on decisive roles of market in resource allocation aims to release new demands and create new supplies; on the one hand, market is supposed to release overcapacity and create new economic growth points, and on the other, the use is made of innovation to form effective supplies with higher quality and stimulate new demands. The supply-side reform is a specific remedy for the currently existing economic issues in China, a new method for China's economic reform and an effective action to vitalize industrial growth.

Firstly, we need to focus on release of excess capacity and elimination of "zombie" enterprises. The existing excess capacity, "zombie" and loss-making enterprises and low-efficiency or even inefficient assets are consuming huge quantity of resources and hinder transformation and upgrading of industrial structure. The Central Economic Working Conference stated expressly that top priority of supply-side structural reform in 2016 would be given to active and prudent dissolution of excess capacity and release of valuable resource elements from enterprises featuring severely excess capacity and limited space for growth and the "zombie" enterprises so as to improve effective supply and create new productivity by straightening out the supply side. To dissolve excess capacity, the Central Government, local government, authorities and enterprises must exercise strict control over incremental productive capacity. In particular, the local government is not supposed to increase investment blindly for local economic development or follow the suit simply because of huge potential in emerging industrials; instead, it should solve this problem at its source. The existing excess productive capacities may be dissolved by carrying out structural optimization or adjustment, promoting enterprise reorganization and M&A, improving inventory warning mechanism and perform real-time monitoring over change in business inventories. Further solutions include: creating external demands and encouraging "go out" of China's industrial capital to promote capacity output under the opportunity of the Belt and Road Initiative, accelerating reform of liberalization of production elements, breaking the government-led distribution mode of land and resources, giving full play to the regulating roles of market mechanism, and guiding allocation of capital and labor in all industrial sectors so as to dissolve excess capacity. As excess capacity is a systematic and long-term issue requiring both short-term administrative intervention and long-term governance according to the law, we need to improve the system of policy, laws and regulations for dissolution of excess capacity, and give full play to fiscal, financial and tax roles in the de-capacity process; accelerate consolidation, reorganization or bankruptcy of "zombie" enterprises or low-efficiency and inefficient assets, and make reasonable relocation of personnel and disposal of assets; actively guide upstream and downstream industrial organizations of the "zombie" enterprises to transform into high value added segments, or accept merging and reorganization of competitive industrial enterprises; and perfect the delisting mechanism of "zombie" enterprises to make adjustment and optimization of industrial structure, providing that the ecological equilibrium of these industrial organizations are maintained.

Secondly, we need to devote great efforts to innovation-driven economy. On the one hand, as innovation and entrepreneur are key supply sides to maintain high-quality, sustainable and vital development of economy, we should comply with the "mass innovation and mass entrepreneurship" strategy and China's Manufacturing Industries 2025 to promote institutional innovation, reinvent government functions, create service-oriented government, improve market mechanism, create a fair, open and transparent competitive environment for all types of market players, adopt competitive policy to guide and stimulate innovation, improve efficiency of resources allocation, streamline administration and delegate power to the lower levels, minimize unnecessary administrative approvals, and enhance vitality and creativity of industrial economics players. 2015 is the year for top design of overall reform and all supporting reform schemes will be implemented in 2016, so we need to pace up institutional reforms in finance, taxation, price and enterprises, take performance of institutional and mechanism reform as core elements in performance appraisal of local government to encourage local government to make innovation and deepen reforms and provide institutional guarantee for operation of industrial enterprises. On the other hand, we should seize the opportunity of the new round of scientific and technological revolution to substantially promote technical innovation, develop new industries; carry out "Internet +" action plan, provide stronger support for new technologies and new products R&D, set up several state-level manufacturing innovation platforms, accelerate transformation of new technologies into practical productivity, actively develop new models, new business types and new products, aim at internationally advanced level, perfect new technical standard system, strengthen brand construction and IPR protection of new products, raise enterprises' concept of independent innovation, encourage enterprises to carry out talent exchange and international training, accelerate formation of reversal mechanism of independent innovation, set up incentive mechanism for enterprises' independent innovation, and pay high attention to development of SMEs' innovation capacity.

Thirdly, we need to foster and carry forward the craftsmanship of "constant pursuit of perfection" and boost transition from "Made in China" to "high-quality manufacturing". Among China's consumer goods, there are currently more than 100 kinds of products that rank first in output around the globe. For instance, the capacity of household appliances, shoemaking, cotton spinning, chemical fiber and wearing apparel takes up over 50% of the global total capacity, and the export of light industry and textile occupy over 30% of the global total export, making China a genuine big power for manufacturing, consumption and export of consumer goods. However, there is still a big gap between China and developed countries in variety structure, product quality and brand cultivation. For this reason, we need to carry on "craftsmanship", carry forward "quality revolution" and guarantee product quality; further improve market access, abrogate unnecessary approval and catalogue and unreasonable changes, carry out strict safety, environment-friendly and energy consumption conditions, provide support for enterprises to make efforts in creative design, technology content and performance, and promote innovation and effective supply of popular consumer goods; actively develop and carry on "craftsmanship" that always seeks for perfect, guide enterprises to establish operation philosophy of "quality first and supreme creditability", boost "quality revolution" based on production of popular consumer goods, and promote transition of "Made in China" to "quality goods manufacturing"; create business environment for fair play, promote domestic consumer goods up to international standards, guide enterprises to strengthen full process quality management from raw materials procurement to production and sales, carry out product certification and third party quality testing, and implement strict recall system of defective products; promote inheritance and upgrading of Chinese time-honored brands, provide support for enterprises to cultivate new brands; strengthen supervision, set up blacklist and huge compensation system for enterprises, improve IPR measures, take severe measures against forged and fake commodities; and constantly improve product quality to raise public credibility and recognition of the quality and brand of domestic consumer goods.

Fourthly, we need to help enterprises to reduce cost and resolve difficulties in development. Since 2015, under the influences of rigid rise in labor cost, rising prices of production factors and high financing cost, many Chinese industrial enterprises are faced with serious difficulties due to continually rising operation cost together with currently sluggish development of industrial economics. The Central Government should issue aid policy to help enterprises overcome these difficulties and avoid large-scale closedown that may lead to adverse impact on economy and society. On the one hand, we need to reduce tax and fee burdens on enterprises, continue with transformation of business tax into value added tax to mitigate tax burden of some of enterprises; enlarge the scope of small and micro-sized enterprises to enjoy half income tax, reduce social insurance changes and streamline all types of insurances into "five basic insurances and one housing reserve"; reduce electricity price and logistic cost; eliminate all unreasonable charges and some administrative charge. Only when all these burdens are brought down can enterprises and especially small and micro-sized enterprises get revitalized and obtain space for innovation. On the other hand, we need to renovate financing methods and increase financial support to solve difficulties in financing, especially for SMEs, and provide current funds for promising and difficult enterprises through comprehensive credit line, buyer's credit and personal credit.

Fifthly and finally, we need to continue with reform of mixed ownership system. The supply-side structural reform aims to further streamline administration and delegate power to the lower levels and optimize services in order to stimulate the market vitality and the social creativity, so the supply-side management is inseparable from reform of state-owned enterprises. Over years the state-owned enterprises have been low in efficiency and short of market vitality, especially in administratively monopolized industries such as petroleum, natural gas, telecommunication and transportation. The mixed ownership system is required by China's socialist market economy system and is also a basic solution to rationalizing the market competition order and to endowing enterprises' macroscopic subjects with equal market positions. Marketization is core to reform of the mixed ownership system. Diversity of the investment subjects or equities that can be realized through introduction of capitals under other ownerships into reform of state-owned enterprises' property system and through improvement of governance mechanism will help stimulate state-owned enterprises' innovation vigor and improve their production efficiency. Therefore, we need to make every endeavor and overcome every difficulty to accelerate reform of the mixed ownership system.

3.3 Expand Effective Demands and Further Exploit Demand-Side's Potentialities to Promote Growth of Industrial Economics

Firstly, we need to make endeavors to promote supply-side reform, but it does not necessarily mean the quit of demand management; instead, implementation of the supply-side reform requires appropriate enlargement of aggregate demands; the supply-side reform and the demand management should promote and cooperate with each other. Since 2015, obstructions have emerged in economic growth measures through expansion of investment and net export volume. The stabilizing and rising consumer goods market is unable to drive industrial growth, but the explosion of various emerging industries due to implementation of the innovation-driven strategy has brought about new possibilities for consumption and investment; as a result, the scale effect was replaced by consumption upgrading and investment efficiency in promoting industrial growth. In addition, the implementation of various regional strategies has provided unprecedented demand space for consumption and trade. In the second quarter of 2016, more effective demands were exploited to promote industrial growth.

Secondly, we need to expand and upgrade consumption. On the one hand, we should focus on development of new technologies and new products, encourage innovation of commercial forms, create new demands by means of new supply, and direct consumers towards intelligent, green and healthy consumption. As the "imitative" consumption period comes to an end, individualized and diversified demand has become the mainstream consumption pattern; therefore, in addition to effort in new commercial forms, we need to make efforts on improvement product quality and grade to accommodate consumers' individualized demands of products, and push consumption towards some new industries. On the other hand, we need to expand consumers' demands by virtue of inter-regional collaboration strategies. As China's economy develops, the consumption potentialities in central and western regions have been exploited to some extent. The current inter-regional collaboration strategy plays an important role in promoting consumption in the underdeveloped central and western regions. The "Yangtze River Economic Belt" is a significant action of China's combination of regional coordination and opening up in the new period. This is an unprecedented policy that links together the eastern, central and western regions, and also a solid step to promote construction of inland economic belts. The western region of China is covered by the Belt and Road Initiative while the developed eastern region will take active part in the strategy by economic ties with central and western regions, and will promote inter-regional interactions through market force. All these will further exploit the consumption potentialities in the central and western regions. Meanwhile, "people foremost" is core to the new-type urbanization; more and more production factors such as rural population, information, capital and technologies that are flooding into cities will generate huge aggregation effect and scale effect in these cities to achieve better development of production factors market, especially the labor market; besides, rural laborers will get better paid in cities and will also improve incomes of urban residents and promote upgrading of consumption structure. Therefore, urbanization is an important means to expand consumption and promote consumption upgrading while the construction of the "Beijing-Tianjin-Hebei integration" and "Yangtze River Economic Belt" provides infinite opportunity for new-type urbanization. The inter-regional connection of public services, social insurance system and transportation will become the main market for future urbanization. To stimulate consumption, we need to make the best of inter-regional collaborative strategy to drive urbanization in the central and western regions; besides, we need to take active measures to optimize consumption environment, standardize market competition to facilitate transition of market competition from quantitative expansion and price competition to quality and differentiation competition, promote service-oriented development of manufacturing enterprises, protect consumers' rights and interests, accelerate infrastructure construction in the field of consumer goods, and implement the "broadband China" strategy.

Thirdly, we need to improve investment efficiency, direct capital into high-efficiency fields, and re-arouse the positive roles of investment in economic growth. On the one hand, we should exploit new potentialities of investment; increase investment in people's livelihood projects, including education, medical treatment, local road construction, rural infrastructure, broadband network lines, information and communication, railway traffic; increase investment in science and technology projects, such as major generic technologies, technologies related to new round of industrial revolution and national defense science and technology; increase investment in environment-friendly projects, such as advanced environment-friendly technology and equipment, environmental protection products and services; and continue with implementation of the Belt and Road Initiative to provide opportunities for Chinese enterprises' going out and new investment methods and further expand investment space. On the other hand, we should reform the financing system. Faced with economic downturn, the Chinese government will inevitably take proactive fiscal policy in 2016. To improve investment efficiency, we need to adjust the methods of financial fund investment in addition to market functions, and make the best of the financial funds in investment; for example, we may set up industrial investment fund and promote PPP mode to accelerate implementation of a group of major projects with outstanding investment benefits, make both the state-owned capital and private capital compete in a fair environment, and motivate vitality of private capitals, which not only will improve the utilization rate and investment efficiency of state-owned capital, but also reduce local government's debts to a large extent. In addition, we should stimulate private investment. The private investment plays critical roles in alleviating local government's investment pressure and debt burdens and providing new kinetic energy for steady economic growth, which requires government authorities to facilitate private capital's access to investment, encourage and guide private capital into more construction fields, create a fair play environment and guarantee equal rights and treatment for both state-owned and private capitals by means of issuing a series of operable policies and systems.

Fourthly and finally, we need to further expand the opening-up fields and increase the trade structure of export commodities. The implementation of the Belt and Road Initiative has ushered in a new pattern of opening up comprehensively and created new external demands for China's foreign trade; currently, however, countries along the Belt and Road Initiative participating in trade with China only involve surrounding countries. The Belt and Road Initiative has provided convenience in trade for China and other countries, and the complementary industries and advantages between China and these countries have provided a good foundation and favorable conditions for further development of future trade. Meanwhile, as China proposes the reindustrialization strategy, global innovation has accelerated and some developed countries have increased integrative development emerging industries such as information technology, new energy, intelligent manufacturing and biology. As a result, the commercialization process of some major technologies has shortened; the trans-boundary integration, industrial breakthrough and remodeling of industrial advantages in all countries have become common phenomena; competition among countries has turned more tense; and homogenization has increased in industries between China and other countries; and developed countries have initiated competition with developing countries in both high-end and traditional industries. This double pressure has brought about severe challenges for China's export trade structure and intends to remold global industrial chain. In the sluggish situation of global economy, therefore, to exploit more export potentialities and seek economic growth in the global industrial chain will require constantly improving the structure, value added and competitiveness of export commodities so that relevant export enterprises will be able to participate in fierce international competition and that achieve practical transition of "Made in China" into "quality manufacturing in China".

Appendix
International Industrial Economics Operation Analysis

International Industries in the First Half of 2016

In the first half of 2016, the world economy was still subject to a deep adjustment period after the financial crisis. Global manufacturing PMI index dropped from 50.1% in April to 50% in May 2016. The industrial economics of major economies recovered slowly in a zigzag way and unevenly in main countries and regions, indicated significant uncertainty in industrial economics operation. In general, developed economies recovered faster than emerging economies did.

A weak recovery continued in developed countries, such as European countries and the United States. The American economy operated fairly well. Due to trade and government investment in consumption that offset slump in consumption, the year-on-year growth rate of American economy was modified to rise by 1.1%, higher than the desired value and the last modified value. The American people's confidence in economy was enhanced by the constantly recovering labor market, the higher employment rate and lower price index. The bounce-off of consumer spending in the second quarter will further promote American GDP growth. In addition, the American industrial production improved markedly. The overall production index (seasonally adjusted) entered year-on-year positive growth status, and the manufacturing PMI has climbed above the threshold since March 2016, which kept ascending on a monthly basis in the first half year and hit a new high in June, so its manufacturing industry was expected to flourish; due to external environment's influence, however, the American trade volume remained in sharp fluctuations, for which there was still large space for improvement. The Eurozone economy recovered slowly, with first quarter's GDP growth rate higher than was expected. The Eurozone industrial production also recovered persistently. The manufacturing PMI in June was the highest this year, which indicated a recovering trend of Eurozone industry. Currently, the inflation pressure was slightly alleviated and generally better than market expectation, and the inflation that had lasted for four months eventually came to an end in June. Eurozone saw a good trend of employment as the unemployment rates kept descending; due to British referendum on departure from the EU and its external environment, however, the Eurozone trade was not as optimistic as expected. Japan suffered a slow economic recovery,

I.E.S.A.T. Institute of Industrial Economics, CASS (ed.), *Summer Report of China Industrial Economic Situation Analysis (2016)*, Current Chinese Economic Report Series, DOI 10.1007/978-981-10-4690-2

regardless of its first quarter's GDP growth rate higher than was expected. Other data indicated that Japanese economy remains flat and that continual fluctuations occurred in its industrial output, e.g. PMI in March stayed below the threshold, inflation risk remained and import/export trade volume kept shrinking.

Among major emerging economies, Brazil's economy and industrial production continued shrinking, but the shrinking amplitude slowed down dramatically; despite a slight decline in the second quarter, Brazil's PMI remained below the threshold in the first half of 2016, with a rising unemployment rate and inflation. In the first quarter, South Africa's economic growth rate went down significantly; the growth rate of industrial production fluctuated drastically; though the PMI began recovering up to the threshold in March, there was still uncertainty in its economic recovery as its inflation deteriorated and foreign trade fluctuated obviously. In comparison, India's economy recovered more steadily, regardless of its sluggish industrial growth. In the first quarter of 2016, India's GDP grew 7.95% year on year, higher than the average of all quarters in 2015, indicating a better recovering trend of India's economy. Since the year of 2016, India's PMI maintained above the threshold; the decreasing amplitude of its foreign trade kept going down and improving steadily. Due to the declining international oil price, Russia's economy continued with the downturn; industrial production remained sluggish, regardless of a slightly positive turnabout. In the first half of 2016, Russia's PMI basically remained below the threshold; the unemployment rate went up somewhat, but the inflation went down markedly and foreign trade improved to some extent. It was clear that as compared with developed economies, major emerging economies were faced with a more difficult problem in economic recovery. In the first half of 2016, the general economic situation of developed economies seemed much better than aforesaid emerging economies.

Developed Economies

(1) The United States

The American GPD growth did quite well in the first half of 2016. According to the latest data issued by the US Department of Commerce, the American GDP in the first quarter amounted to US$ 16.51 trillion and the actual year-on-year growth rate was modified to be 1.1%, higher than the expected value and higher than 0.8% of the last modification value; whereas, the American GDP grew 0.6, 3.9, 2 and 1.4% respectively in four quarters last year. This indicated that the American economic outlook was improving, and that the personal consumption expenditure stimulated month-on-month GDP growth by 1.02 percentage points (seasonally adjusted), which was 1.19, 2.42, 2.04 and 1.66 percentage points in four quarters last years. The total American domestic private investment stimulated month-on-month GDP growth by −0.29 percentage point (seasonally adjusted), which was 1.39, 0.85, −0.11 and −0.16 percentage points respectively in four quarters last year. The commodity and service export stimulated month-on-month GDP growth by 0.04 percentage point (seasonally adjusted), which was −0.81, 0.64, 0.09 and −0.25 percentage points in four quarters last year. The government consumption expenditure and total investment stimulated month-on-month GDP growth by 0.23 percentage point (seasonally adjusted), which was 0.01, 0.46, 0.32 and 0.02 percentage points in four quarters last year. It is thus clear that the improvement of American government consumption expenditure and investment in the first quarter has offset the flat consumption expenditure and sustained the overall economic performance to certain extent, and that the rebounding consumption expenditure in the second quarter will further accelerate and remain the main motive force to stimulate the American GDP growth. The initial value of Michigan's American consumer confidence index in June slightly dropped to 94.3, better than the expected 94.0. However, the British referendum on departure from the EU that added much too global economic uncertainty will also compromise the American economic recovery process to a large extent.

By and large, the American labor market saw a moderate recovering trend. In January and February 2016, the American unemployment rate was 4.9% (seasonally adjusted), the lowest since May 2008. In March and April, it was 5.0% (seasonally adjusted), slightly rising as against the first months. The labor participation rate was 62.7, 62.9, 63 and 62.8% respectively in four months, higher than monthly data in the second half of 2015. The population first applying for unemployment compensation in mid-March 2016 dropped to 259,000 persons, which was the minimum level since mid-October last year and lower than the mid-value of 275,000 persons and last period value of 278,000 persons; meanwhile, the population continuing to enjoy unemployment compensation also dropped to a new record low. In May 2016, the American unemployment rate (seasonally adjusted) further dropped to 4.7%, a new low since May 2008. This indicates that the American employment is getting better and better.

The American industrial growth saw an obvious uptrend and the PMI in June 2016 reached a new peak in a year. In the first quarter of 2016, the general industrial production index (seasonally adjusted) of the United States maintained a negative year-on-year growth rate and a declining month-on-month growth rate. The American industrial production index was 103.38 in March, but the year-on-year growth rate turned positive in April, with the year-on-year growth rates in April and May being 0.1% and 0.0% respectively. In the first half year, the capacity utilization rate of all American industrial sectors maintained at about 75%; in November 2016, the American PMI dropped below 50 for the first time since November 2012; from December 2012 to February 2016, the American PMI remained below 50; in February 2016, PMI was 49.50, rising by 2.7 percentage points over January; in March, PMI first climbed up to 51.80 after staying below the threshold for consecutive four years, rising by 2.3 percentage points over February. Since March, the American PMI has stayed above the threshold and kept ascending on a monthly basis in the first half of 2016; in June, PMI was up to 53.2, the highest since February 2015, and the employment rate climbed over the threshold value of 50 for the first time. The American manufacturing industry also recovered faster and faster, and was expected to flourish.

The American inflation rate remained low after fluctuations. Due to seasonal factors, the American oil price ascended in January, and the CPI grew 1.4% year on year, higher than 0.7% in December 2015 and the highest since October 2014. The core CPI grew 2.2% year on year, higher than 2.1% of the growth rate in last period and the highest since June 2012. In February and May, however, it declined and maintained at a low level 1 and 0.9% respectively. In January 2016, the American PPI (final demand, seasonally adjusted) decreased 0.3% year on year; in February, it stayed flat with the same period; in March, it dropped 0.1% year on year, indicating that the PPI kept decreasing at a slow rate; in April, it grew 0.1% year on year; in May, it stayed flat with the same period again. The constantly declining unemployment rate and price index boosted the American people's confidence in economy.

Under the influence of external environment, the American trade witnessed sharp fluctuations. In the first half of 2016, the American import volume and export volume saw a negative year-on-year growth rate, with the year-on-year numerical fluctuation of import fluctuating obviously more drastically than the fluctuation of export. In February, the American export grew −4.19% while the import grew 0.31% year on year; and in May, the export grew −4.21% while the import grew −3.05% year on year. The American trade deficit was unsteady. In March 2016, the trade deficit increased 26.26% year on year; in May, it declined 2.42% year on year, with the total export volume (seasonally adjusted) amounting to US$ 182.354 billion, increasing US$ 314 million as against the previous month, and the total import volume (seasonally adjusted) amounting to US$ 223.498 billion, increasing US$ 347.7 million as against the previous month.

(2) Eurozone

The Eurozone economy recovered slowly. In the first quarter of 2016, the month-on-month final value of seasonally adjusted GDP in Eurozone was revised from 0.5% up to 0.6% while the year-on-year final value was revised from 1.5% up to 1.7%, higher than the market expectation and obviously higher than 0.2% of the fourth quarter of 2015; however, the recovering foundation still needed to consolidation. The household consumption expenditure of EU 27 nations stimulated month-on-month GDP growth by 0.36%, the gross capital formation did 0.23%, the commodity and service export did 0.16%, and export did −0.34%. Among the three major economies in Eurozone, France's gross domestic product (current price, seasonally adjusted) grew 2.35% year on year, lower than 2.62 and 2.70% respectively in the third and fourth quarters of 2015. Germany's economic growth improved to some extent; in the first quarter, the month-on-month initial value of German GDP was 0.6%, higher than 0.32% of the fourth quarter in 2015. As EU's main trade partners' economic growth slowed down and the positive factors reversed, the *Economic Forecast in Spring 2016* issued by EU predicted that its economic growth rates in 2016 and 2017 would continue to increase (1.8 and 1.9%

respectively), but the increasing amplitude would be lower than its Winter forecast (1.9 and 2.0% respectively).

The unemployment rate kept falling. In the first half of 2016, the unemployment rate of the Eurozone continued with the continuous downtrend of 2015. The Eurozone unemployment rate (seasonally adjusted) was 10.2% in April and further dropped to 10.1% in May, decreasing 0.1 percentage point as against April, the lowest since February 2012.

The industrial production continually recovered during fluctuations. In March 2016, the industrial production index of Eurozone 17 nations (seasonally adjusted) grew 3.1% year on year and 2.1% month on month, higher than 1.7% of market expectation, including month-on-month growth of 3.9% of capital goods output, 2.4% of energy goods output, 2.3% of consumer goods output and 0.9% of intermediate goods output, obviously higher than growth rates in recent half year. In February, it grew 1% year on year, a positive growth rate for consecutive fourteen months but decreasing 2.1 percentage points year on year and 0.94 percentage point month on month as against the year-on-year growth rate in the previous month. In the first quarter of 2016, the Eurozone's capacity utilization rate was 81.2%, decreasing 0.2 percentage point as against the fourth quarter of 2015; in the second quarter, it was 81.4%, rising by 0.2 percentage point over the previous quarter. In December 2015, the Eurozone's PMI was 53.2, increasing 0.4 over the previous month for consecutive four months and reaching a new high in the past twenty months; from January to May 2016, it dropped again to 51.5 in May, decreasing 0.2 as against April; in June, however, it ascended to 52.80, higher than the initial value of 52.6 and the highest value this year. The accelerating industrial production indicated that the Eurozone's economy kept recovering.

The inflationary pressure slowed down but still existed. The year-on-year final value of the Eurozone's CPI was 0.3, −0.2 and 0.0% respectively from January to March 2016, and −0.2, −0.1 and 0.1% respectively from April to June, generally better than market expectation; the inflationary state that lasted for consecutive four months was terminated in June largely due to rising energy prices and recovering internal demands. The year-on-year final value of core CPI was 0.7, 0.8 and 0.9% respectively. In addition, Germany saw 0.3% and France saw 0.2% year-on-year final value of CPI in June; the PPI persisted in falling. In June 2016, the Eurozone 17 nations' PPI decreased 3.85% year on year, 0.52 percentage point lower than May. The Eurozone's PPI has kept decreasing year on year for consecutive 35 months since August 2013.

Sharp fluctuations occurred in Eurozone's trade volume, foreboding a pessimistic prospect. From January to April 2016, the Eurozone 18 nations' import volume grew −1, 1.9, −8.4 and −5.3% respectively, lower than 4.4 and 3.5% in November and December 2015; their export volume grew −2.1, 1.2, −2.3 and −0.9% respectively, lower than 6.3% and 4.15 respectively in November and December 2015. Their trade surplus kept shrinking, too. In April 2016, the Eurozone 18 nations' trade surplus (seasonally adjusted) amounted to €27.482 billion, reduced by €1.946 billion as against March, with total export volume (seasonally adjusted) amounting to €172.313 billion, reduced by €6.289 billion as against the previous month, and total import volume (seasonally adjusted) amounting to €144.831 billion, reduced by €4.344 billion as against the previous month. The shrinking trade surplus was mainly caused by smaller export volume and larger amplitude.

(3) Japan

The annualized and seasonally adjusted month-on-month initial value of Japan's GDP was 1.7% in the first quarter, significantly higher than the median 0.3% of market expectation and −1.7% of previous value, but other economic data of Japan remained flat. Japan's unemployment rate declined slightly. Japan's unemployment rate (seasonally adjusted) was 3.2, 3.3 and 3.2% respectively in January, February and March 2016, and maintained at 3.2% in April and May, slightly lower than the average of four quarters in 2015.

Japan's industrial output fluctuated constantly. From January to May 2016, the industrial production index of Japan's mining industry and manufacturing industry (seasonally adjusted) grew −4.16, −1.15, 0.19, −3.33 and −0.11% year on year respectively. In April 2016, Japan's capacity utilization rate index was 96.5, decreasing 4.33% year on year and 12.4% month on month. Japan's PPI kept declining below the threshold. In February 2016, Japan's PPI was 50.1, decreased by 2.2 as against January 2016, and it dropped again after an uptrend for a while. In March, Japan's PPI dropped to 49.1, exceeding the expectation and decreased by 1 as against February 2016, and it further dropped below the threshold after staying around the threshold for a while; from April to June, it remained below the threshold.

The inflationary risk still existed in Japan. Since the super easing monetary policy was implemented in Japan in 2013, the inflation continued to maintain at a low level. In January and February 2016, Japan's CPI grew 0 and 0.3% year on year respectively, and the core CPI grew 0.0% year on year. In March, due to decreasing oil prices and slowdown of the rising durable goods prices and overseas tourist prices, Japan's CPI decreased 0.1% and the core CPI decreased 0.3% as compared with the same period last year, the largest decreasing amplitude since April 2014; meanwhile, the PPI also kept decreasing. In March 2016, Japan's PPI decreased 3.775 year on year, a decrease for consecutive eleven months, and the decreasing amplitude would intensify in March. In April and May, the decreasing amplitude of PPI further intensified, decreased by 4.25 and 4.24% year on year respectively. However, the shrinking inflation failed to stimulate Japan's Central Bank to carry out new easing policy after its implementation of negative interest rate in February 2016.

Japan's trade volume continued shrinking. Since the fourth quarter of 2015, Japan's export volume suffered a negative year-on-year growth rate; in the first half of 2016, Japan's export volume continued with the trend of negative growth and the amplitude seemed to intensify, growing −12.86, −3.99 and −6.78% year on year respectively from January to March and −6.78, −10.07 and −11.27% year on year respectively from April to June. Japan's import volume also suffered a negative growth rate, growing −17.84, −14.18 and −14.93% year on year respectively from

January to March and −14.85, −23.29 and −13.80% year on year respectively from April to June, which indicated an intensifying amplitude of negative growth. Japan's overall trade surplus turned into a deficit in May after rising from February to April; the deficit amounted to JPY40.7 billion, including JPY63.2 billion of import volume increased over the previous month and JPY789.6 billion of export volume decreased from the previous month. Japan's trade deficit was mainly caused by drastic decline of export volume (Figs. A.1, A.2 and A.3).

Emerging Economies

(1) Brazil

Brazil economy continued shrinking, but the amplitude slowed down. From January to March 2016, Brazil's GDP grew −8.95, −9.29 and −9.37% year on year respectively, significantly reduced as compared with −28% year-on-year growth rate in the fourth quarter of 2015. A year-on-year growth rate of 2.72% was realized in the first quarter, lower than growth rates in all quarters of 2015.

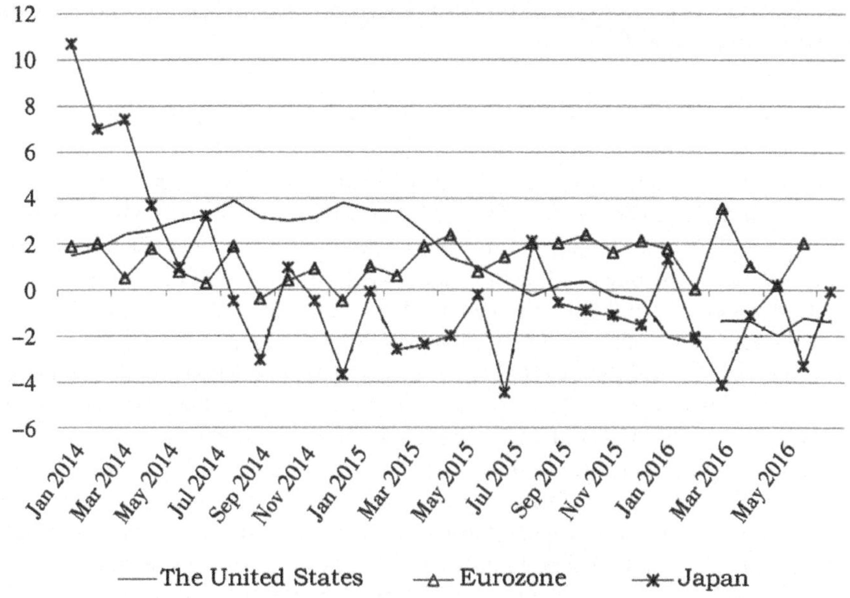

Fig. A.1 Year-on-year growth rates of the industrial production index in main developed countries (*unit %*). *Data source* Wind Information database. *Notes* Indicators used to calculate year-on-year growth rates include American overall industrial output index (seasonally adjusted), Eurozone 19 nations' industrial production index and Japan's mining and manufacturing industrial production index

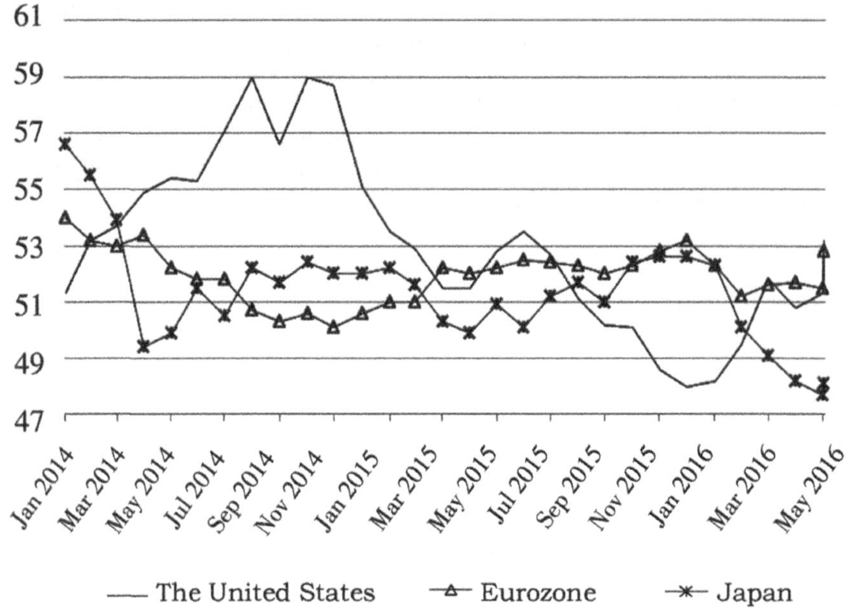

Fig. A.2 PMI index of main developed countries. *Data source* Wind Information database. *Notes* Indicators used include American ISM's manufacturing PMI, Eurozone manufacturing PMI and Japanese manufacturing PMI

Brazil's industrial production saw negative growth rates. From January to May 2016, Brazil's industrial production index decreased 13.6, 9.6, 11.5, 6.9 and 7.8% year on year respectively, which lasted for consecutive 27 months since March 2014, but the decreasing amplitude retarded slowly, and grew −1.3, −0.52, 10.29, −0.96% and 3.74% month on month respectively. The manufacturing PMI remained below the threshold; in November 2015, Brazil's PMI decreased to 43.8, the lowest since April 2009; in December 2015 and January 2016, the PMI picked up but decreased again to 44.5 in February 2016, decreasing 2.9 as against the previous month. In March, the PMI climbed up to 46, still below the threshold but rising by 1.5 over the previous month; in the second quarter, the PMI remained at low level, i.e. 42.6, 41.6 and 43.2 respectively in three months.

The unemployment rate continued climbing. In October 2015, Brazil's unemployment rate was 7.9% in six major cities, the highest since September 2009; but it decreased for a short time in November and December 2015. In January 2016, the unemployment rate climbed again to 7.6%, rising by 0.7% over the previous month. In February, it continued going up to 8.2%, rising by 0.6 percentage point over the previous month and the highest since September 2009.

Brazil's inflation was expected to rise. From January to March 2016, the general CPI in Brazil grew 10.71%, 10.36% and 9.39% year on year respectively, staying at a high level. Brazil's PPI also kept rising. In February 2016, the PPI grew 13.56%

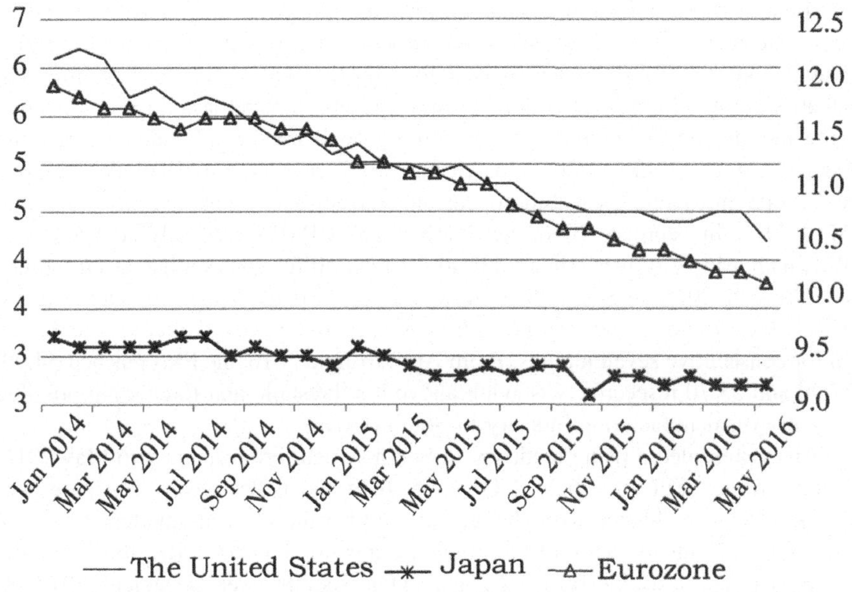

Fig. A.3 Unemployment rates of main developed countries. *Data source* Wind Information database. *Notes* American and Japanese data are indicated on the *left* coordinate axis and Eurozone's data on the *right* coordinate axis. Indicators used include unemployment rates (seasonally adjusted) from Eurozone, Japan and the United States

year on year, rising by 1.72 percentage points over January; the year-on-year growth rate of PPI accelerated on a monthly basis in all months but December 2015 since March 2015, and hit the peak value in February 2016 since May 2015. In March, the PPI grew 13.03%, decreasing by 0.53 percentage point as against February but presenting a slowdown trend. Brazil's trade surplus also fluctuated sharply. In January 2016, Brazil's trade surplus amounted to US$ 923 million, decreased by US$ 5.317 billion as against December 2015; in February 2016, it amounted to US$ 3.043 billion, increased by US$ 2.12 billion over January; in June, it amounted to US$ 3.983 billion, decreased by US$ 6.461 billion as against May, including US$ 1.635 billion of import volume increased over the previous month and US$ 827 million of export volume decreased from the previous month. The shrinking trade surplus in Brazil was caused mainly by the fact that the increment of import volume outnumbered the export volume.

(2) South Africa

South Africa's economy saw a significant drop. In the first quarter, its GDP grew −0.16%, where private consumers' expenditure took up about 60% of GDP and stimulated GDP to grow 0.52 percentage point. The generally steady private consumption was the main reason for the fact that South Africa's economy did not fall into depression or recession.

South Africa's industrial production growth suffered sharp fluctuations and its economic recovery remained uncertain. In October 2015, the manufacturing production index of South Africa (seasonally adjusted) turned for the first time into negative growth from positive year-on-year growth that had lasted for consecutive three months, and maintained the negative growth trend until January 2016 and reached 106.8 in February 2016, increasing 0.37% year on year. The index dropped to −1.84% in March, presenting a year-on-year negative value, and grew 1.8% in April 2016. In February 2016, the South Africa's PMI (seasonally adjusted) was 47.1, increasing 3.6 over January but lower than 50 for consecutive seven months since August 2015. In March 2016, however, the PMI reached 50.5, increasing 2.6 over February and for the first time climbing up to the threshold after staying below 50 for consecutive seven months. From April to June 2016, the PMI reached 54.90, 51.90 and 53.70 respectively, staying above the threshold and foreboding possible recovery of manufacturing industry in South Africa.

Prices presented a rising tendency in South Africa. From January to May 2016, South Africa's CPI grew 6.23, 7.00, 6.55, 6.49 and 6.48% year on year respectively, obviously higher than the average CPI values in all quarters of 2015. Meanwhile, South Africa's PPI continued rising. In January 2016, the PPI grew 7.6% year on year, increasing 2.8 percentage points over December 2015; in February, the PPI grew 8.1% year on year, increasing 0.5 percentage point over January; from March to May, the PPI declined slightly as against February, but remained at around 7%, higher than the average in all months of 2015.

South Africa's trade volumes fluctuated sharply. From January to May 2016, South Africa's export value grew 6.46, 18.13, 4.83, 8.09 and 17.85% year on year respectively, generally higher than 3.27, 11.06 and 0.92% from October to December 2015, and its import value grew −2.11, 7.53, 2.58, 6.43 and 2.46% year on year respectively. In October 2015, South Africa's trade surplus amounted to 21.4 billion Rand, increased by 20.1 billion Rand over September. South Africa's trade saw a short-time surplus in November and December 2015, but suffered a deficit of 17.871 billion Rand in January 2016, with 16.574 billion Rand of export decreased as against the previous month and 8.857 billion Rand of import increased over the previous month. In February, South Africa's trade deficit amounted to 1.267 billion Rand, shrinking by 7.59 billion Rand as against January; from March to May, its trade balance amounted to 2.034 billion Rand, −127 million Rand and 18.731 billion Rand respectively.

(3) India

In the first quarter of 2016, India's GDP grew 7.95% year on year, higher than the average in all quarters of 2015 and indicating a better trend of India's economic recovery; the growth of India's GDP was driven by consumption, which contributed 4.9% to India's economic growth or took up 62% of India's economic aggregate.

As compared with other emerging economies, India's industry remained flat but recovered steadily. In October 2015, India's industrial production index grew 9.8% year on year, a positive growth rate for consecutive twelve months and the highest in recent five years; from November 2015 to January 2016, however, India's industrial production suffered a negative year-on-year growth rate for three months and eventually rebounded to1.99% in February 2016, presenting uptrend of year-on-year growth of industrial production. India's PMI continued rising. In December 2015, the PMI was 49.1, decreasing below the threshold for the first since 2014; in 2016, however, it remained above the threshold. In June, India's PMI reached 51.7, decreased by 1 over May.

From January to May 2016, India's consumer price index of industrial workers grew 5.91, 5.53, 5.51, 5.86 and 6.59% year on year respectively, generally lower than 6.32, 6.72 and 6.32% from October to December 2015. However, India's PPI started rising; in March 2016, India's WPI decreased 0.85% year on year, a negative growth rate for consecutive seventeen months, but the decreasing rate slowed down on a monthly basis; in May and June, the PPI saw a positive year-on-year growth rate, i.e. 0.34 and 0.79%.

The year-on-year decreasing growth rate of India's foreign trade retarded. From January to May 2016, India's total export volume grew −13.57, −5.46, −5.16, −6.62 and −0.79% year on year respectively, with the decreasing amplitude obviously less than −17.16, −26.27 and −13.92% from October to December 2015; India's total import volume grew −10.85, −5.06, −23.80, −24.15 and −13.16% year on year respectively, with the decreasing amplitude also less than the average of three months in the fourth quarter of 2015. This indicated that India's foreign trade was improving and that its foreign trade deficit was getting less and less. From January to May 2016, India managed to keep trade deficit below US$ 10 billion and lower than the deficit in the fourth quarter of 2015. India's trade deficit was mainly caused by the considerable decrement of its export volume.

(4) Russia

Since 2015, the continually falling international oil prices has led to a fast setback in Russia's foreign exchange earnings and the seriously insufficient funds for economic development has resulted in Russia's economic slump. In March 2016, Russia's GDP decreased 1.8% year on year. Regardless of somewhat uptrend, Russia's industrial production remained sluggish. In January 2016, Russia's industrial production index (seasonally adjusted) decreased 2.59% year on year, a negative year-on-year growth rate for consecutive twelve months; since February, however, all months saw a positive growth rate except March when the index decreased 0.36% year on year. Since 2016, Russia's PMI has kept shrinking but stayed above the threshold; in June, however, the PMI reduced to 51.5%, below the threshold.

Russia's unemployment rate kept going up. After seasonal adjustment, Russia's unemployment rate jumped to 6%, rising by 0.2 percentage point per monthly in March 2016, which hit a new high since January 2013 and ended the four-month period in which the rate remained at 5.8%, and it also stayed at 5.9%, higher than market expectation. In this period, Russia's total unemployment increased to 4.567 million people, rising by 138,000 people per month, which was also higher than 4.503 million people in the same period last year. Russia's labor-force participation rate jumped to 68.9%, rising by 0.2 percentage point per month. Russia's CPI and PPI growth rates kept slowing down; from January to May 2016, Russia's CPI grew 9.8, 8.1, 7.3, 7.3 and 7.5% year on year respectively, generally lower than the average of all months in 2015; from March to May, Russia's PPI grew 0.8, 0.9 and 3.2% year on year respectively, obviously lower than the average of all months in 2015.

Russia's foreign trade improved somewhat. From January to April 2016, Russia's foreign export goods grew −38.8, −31.70, −29.3 and −28.8% year on year respectively, with the decreasing amplitude slightly narrowing as compared to each month in 2015; meanwhile, Russia's import grew −19.0, −16.4, −10.3 and −6.5% year on year respectively, with the decreasing amplitude obviously slowing down. In general, Russia's foreign trade surplus was faced with a limited space for improvement. In April 2016, Russia's trade surplus amounted to US$ 6.752 billion, decreasing US$ 1.178 billion as against March, including US$ 1.401 billion of export volume and US$ 223 million of import volume decreased against the previous month (Figs. A.4, A.5 and A.6).

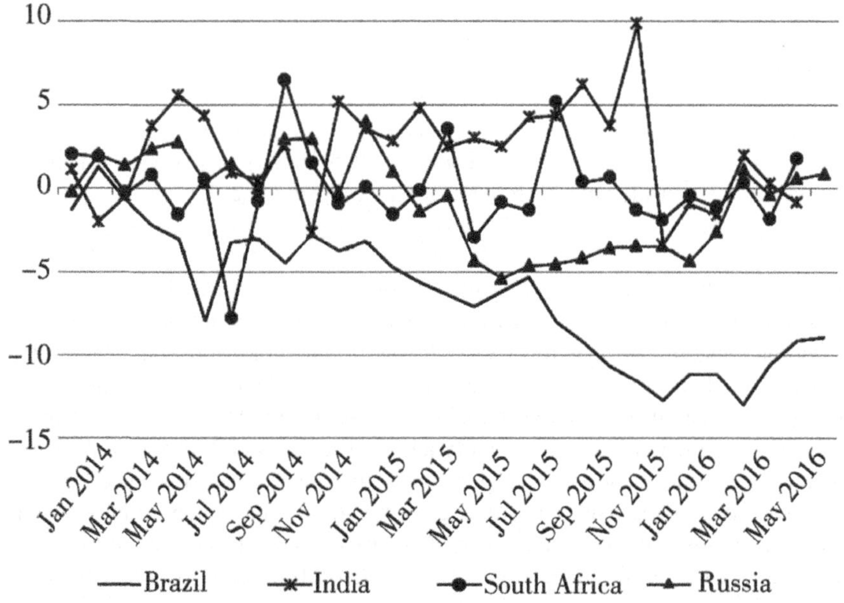

Fig. A.4 Year-on-year growth rates of main emerging economies' industrial production index (*unit %*). *Data source* Wind Information database. *Notes* Indexes used to calculate year-on-year growth rates include India's industrial production index (2004–2005 = 100), Brazil's industrial production index (seasonally adjusted, 2012 = 100), South Africa's all manufacturing production indexes (seasonally adjusted, 2010 = 100) and Russia's industrial production index (2010 = 100)

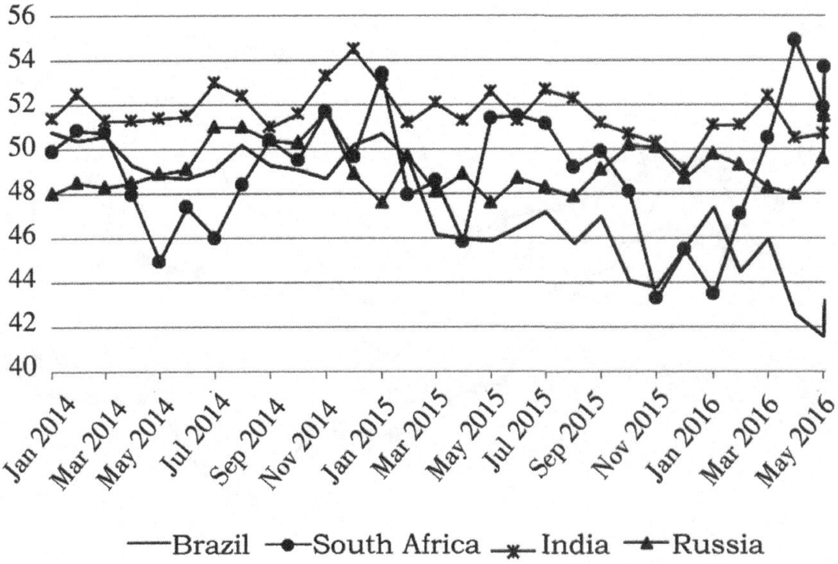

Fig. A.5 Main emerging economies' manufacturing PMIs. *Data source* Wind Information database. *Notes* Indexes used include India's manufacturing PMI, Brazil's manufacturing PMI, South Africa's PMI (seasonally adjusted) and Russia's manufacturing PMI

Prospect of International Industry in the Second Half of 2016

Due to slow recovery of developed economies and sluggish growth of emerging economies, the prospect of global economic growth remains weak. The Federal Reserve's increase of interest rates in December 2015 has produced prodigious influence on the world economy; meanwhile, the influence of strong dollar policy and the Federal Reserve's constant intensification of interest rate hike expectation will persist in the second half of 2016, which may cause a further turmoil in global economy. Under such a background, all other main economies than the United States begin to exercise easing policy, differentiating global policies and adding much to uncertainties and risks of global economic recovery. The effects of British departure from the EU will manifest step by step and aggravate uncertainties in global economic recovery and the Central Bank's policy. In February 2016, OECD cut the global economic forecast for 2016 down to 3.0% (previously 3.3%) and also sharply down-regulated the economic growth expectations of main developed economies. For economic prospect in the second half of 2016, the world economy will recover slowly, with persisting regional differentiation, and the developed economies will perform better than emerging economies; however, the global economy will still be faced with many uncertainties.

It is predicted that the growth rate of developed economies in the second half of 2016 will slow down in stabilization. As the economic fundamentals of the United

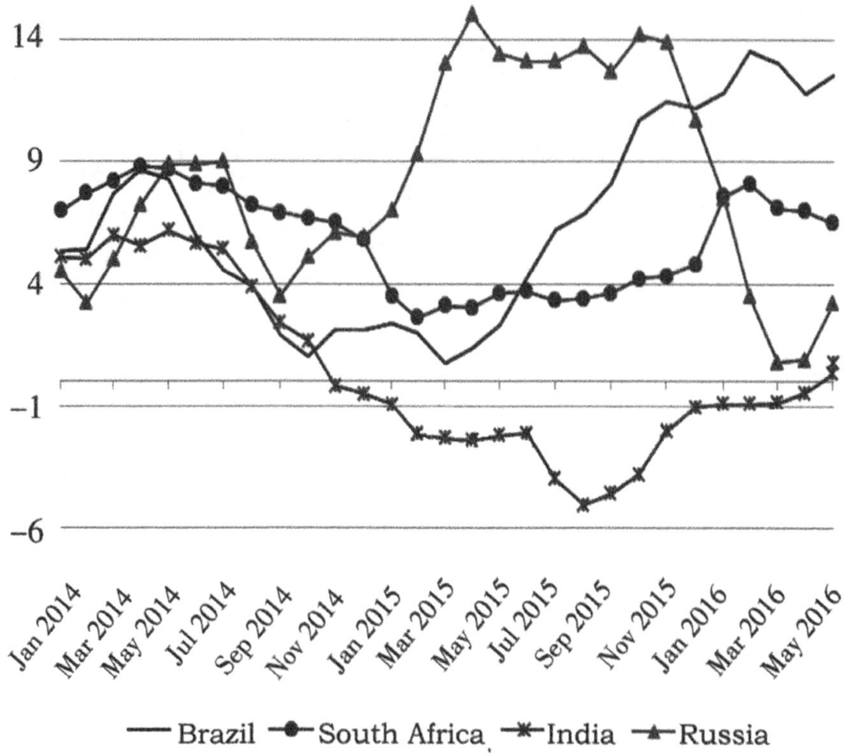

Fig. A.6 Year-on-year growth rates of Main emerging economies' PPIs (*unit %*). *Data source* Wind Information database. *Notes* Indexes used include Brazil's IPA—year-on-year M—monthly, South Africa's PPI of industrial products/finished products—year-on-year—monthly, India's WPI—all commodities—year-on-year—monthly, and Russia's PPI—year-on-year—monthly

States are superior to most main economies and the recovering trend of American economy remains unchanged, the steady growth of consumption expenditure will be one of the definite motive powers for American economic recovery. Although the American economy is unlikely to break through the annual average growth rate of 2.2% in future several years since financial crisis under the influences of aging population and slowing growth of labor productivity, it is noted that the American total factor productivity is improving persistently to accumulate strengths for comprehensive economic recovery. After the Federal Reserve's FOMC meeting in March 2016, the Federal Reserve kept current interest rate unchanged in consistence with market expectations; after the interest rate is raised, the Federal Reserve still maintained that "the Federal fund rate may be lower than the expected long-term level in a given period, but the actual path will depend on the economic prospect indicated by future data" for future increase of interest rate. According to the Federal Reserve's FORMC meeting in June 2016, the British referendum and labor data in May added much to the uncertainty, which widened disagreements among the Federal Reserve; the market analysts argued that it would be less likely to raise interest rate by the end of 2016; in addition, the American general election will be there in 2016 and requires conservative monetary policies, so it is less likely for the Federal Reserve to raise interest rate in the second half of 2016. While the world economic upheaval due to the Federal Reserve's increase of interest rate at the end of 2015 could weaken gradually prior to next increase of interest rate, the Federal Reserve's increase of interest rate in 2016 would be a time bomb. The American economy may pick up after the flood in Mississippi River basin, but its economic activities in the second half of 2016 will be more or less affected by the flood. Continuous economic recovery after the crisis may facilitate gradual recovery of American capacity, but the bottleneck of capacity recovery will undermine acceleration of American industrial production. When other main economies in the world continue with easing monetary policies, the US dollar will further appreciate and bring down American export and thus cause adverse influence on American economic growth; all these influences along with uncertainties in global economy and financial situation will put American economic recovery at risk.

It is also predicted that the Eurozone's economic recovery will be sluggish. The European Central Bank's decision on monetary policy in March 2016 startled the market. It decided to down-regulate three key interest rates: the deposit rate from −0.30 to −0.40%, the main refinancing rate from 0.05 to 0.00% (the first time since September 2014) and the marginal lending rate from 0.30 to 0.25%, and increased the debt purchase size to €80 billion. The easing monetary policy may reduce enterprises' loan cost and promote recovery of real economy, the stimulating effect of easing monetary policy will weaken significantly as time goes on; besides, some deep-seated problems, such as unsmooth transmission of the banking system and dislocation of labor force population, will be resolved simply by monetary policy. Sustainable recovery of Eurozone's economic growth requires joint efforts from a series of monetary and fiscal policies. Greece's break of contract and Britain's referendum intensified market's uncertainty in Eurozone's prospect and will lead to some adverse results in the second half of 2016. With stabilizing oil price, the deflationary risk will narrow and the long-term deflationary pressure will ease, but they will remain the biggest risk of Eurozone's economy; meanwhile, the sluggish demand of China-led emerging markets will also produce certain risks for Eurozone's export volume.

It is predicted that there will remain uncertainties about Japan's economic recovery in the second half of 2016. At the end of January 2016, the Central Bank of Japan unexpectedly announced exercise of negative interest rate, maintained JPY80 trillion of annual QQE, and postponed the time to realize 2% inflation target into the first half of 2017 fiscal year. After exercise of negative interest rate, however, the changes in Japan's finance implied more uncertainties because the negative interest rate produced adverse effects on Japanese financial institutions while stimulating economic growth. In March 2016, the Central Bank of Japan decided to maintain the existing policy of −0.1% negative interest rate and the plan on annual increment of JPY80 trillion for monetary base, intentionally awaiting the further results after exercise of the negative interest rate policy. Continuous appreciation of Japanese Yen offset part of rising prices of bulk commodities and did no good to Japan's imported inflation and export, which would force the Central Bank of Japan to maintain easing monetary policy. Therefore, Japan's economic recovery will depend largely on the Central Bank's policy; however, if the economic growth rates decline sharply in the Asia-Pacific region due to sluggish economic growth of China and the US Federal Reserve's re-raise of interest rates, the Japan's economy will be subject to serious impact.

The emerging markets and the developing economies are expected to stabilize or even pick up, though the process may be rather rough. Many countries have developed programs and measures to promote economic recovery. This also leads to differentiated recovery processes. India sees a promising prospect of economic recovery. The "Made in India" program proposed by Indian Government aims to increase manufacturing industry's proportion in India's gross domestic product and create more jobs by increasing budgetary outlays for investment in infrastructure construction, lowering the upper limit for foreign direct investment, cutting down on government subsidies and reducing taxes on enterprises. Implementation of the program and manifestation of its effects will further help overall recovery of India's economy. Under the influence of weak private investment in India and external economic context, India's economic recovery will be faced with various hardships. According to BMI Research's prediction in March 2016, India's economy will grow 7.2% during 2016 and 2017, which is lower than the 7.6% growth rate predicted by the Central Statistical Organization; the recovery process of developed countries will be slow; no significant improvement will be made in European and American economy; main emerging countries' economy will remain in deep water; Brazil's economy will suffer a serious recession and difficult recovery due to deteriorating external environment, rising unemployment rate and prices, higher indebtedness and the current political crisis; the likelihood of US Federal Reserve's raise of interest rates at the end of 2015 will persist, and capital outflows caused thereby will produce more pressure on emerging economies with lower foreign exchange reserves, such as South Africa, whose economy will be faced with severe challenges from large-scale declining prices of market assets and currently serious domestic inflation; and Russia's economic prospect also seems not as optimistic as expected. Regard to Russia's economic growth in 2016, the International Monetary Fund (IMF) predicted a decrease of 1%, the World Bank predicted a decrease of 0.7%, and the international rating agency Fitch Ratings down-regulated Russia's growth forecast of growing 0.5% to decreasing 1%. On March 1st, 2016, Russia issued the 2016 Action Plan for Steady Development of Social Economy, i.e. the Anti-Crisis Plan, to promote recovery of real economy. In the short run, the emerging markets are still under the adverse influences of fluctuating prices of bulk commodities and drastic appreciation of US dollar, but the medium-term risk facing emerging markets still lies in Chinese economy's "hard landing" or potential significant slowdown or more universal spillover effects due to potential growth.

The manufacturer's authorised representative in the EU is Springer Nature Customer Service Centre GmbH, Europaplatz 3, 69115 Heidelberg, Germany. If you have any concerns regarding our products, please contact ProductSafety@springernature.com

Printed and bound by CPI Group (UK) Ltd, Croydon, CR0 4YY

30/09/2026

02225465-0002